You Had Me at Bow Wow

"Yes, yes, yes, I miss you, too, honey. Now put the dog on."

You Had Me at Bow Wow

A Book of Dog Cartoons

Jack Ziegler

The Vendome Press

ACKNOWLEDGMENTS

*Thanks to Christopher Sweet, Bob Mankoff, Jane Cavolina,
The Cartoon Bank, Misha, and Blanche.*

First published in the United States of America by
The Vendome Press
1334 York Avenue
New York, N.Y. 10021

Twenty-eight of the drawings reproduced in this book were first published in The New Yorker magazine.

Library of Congress Cataloging-in-Publication Data

Ziegler, Jack.
  You had me at bow wow : a book of dog cartoons / Jack Ziegler.
    p. cm.
 ISBN-13: 978-0-86565-177-7
 ISBN-10: 0-86565-177-9
 1. Dogs--Caricatures and cartoons. 2. American wit and humor, Pictorial.
I. Title.
 NC1429.Z47A4 2006
 741.5'6973--dc22

                         2006009608

2006 2007 2008 2009 / 10 9 8 7 6 5 4 3 2 1

Designed by Véronique Lefèvre-Sweet

Printed and bound in China

For Holden Casey, who will one day get his dog.

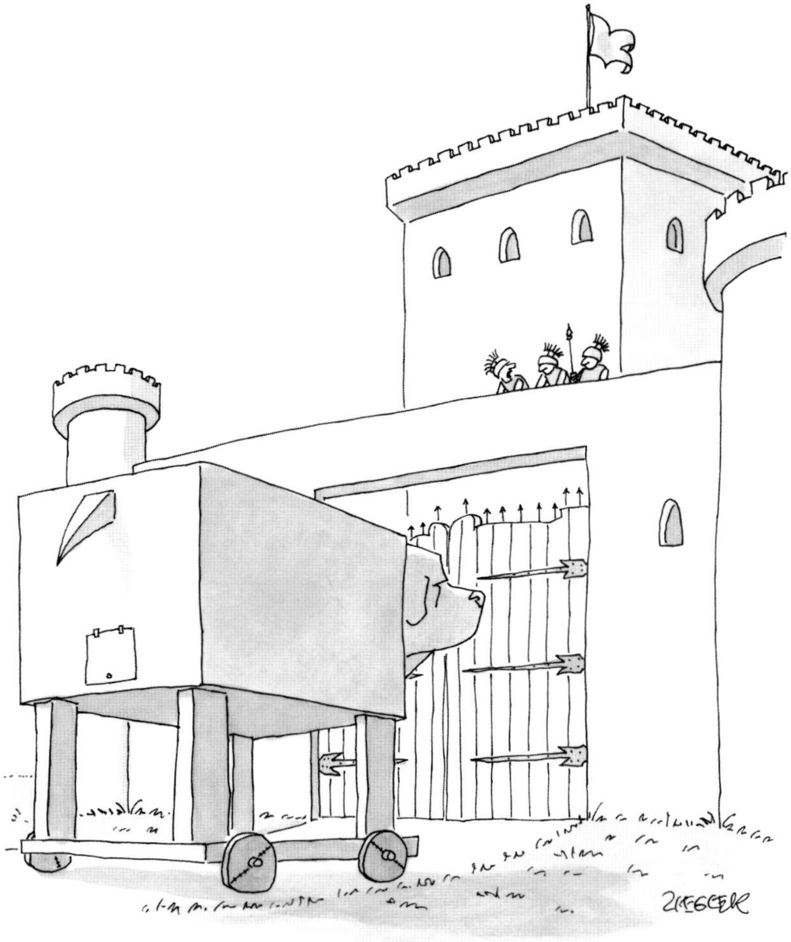
ZIEGLER

"You're right, sir—it is cute. But the last time we let one of these things in the entire kingdom was overrun with ticks, mites, and fleas."

*"It all started with a couple of simple dog tricks and, before I knew it,
I had an agent, a set of eight-by-ten glossies and thirty-six of these fabulous caps."*

Introduction

We read a notice in the paper that the Las Vegas pound was giving away free dogs (cutting inventory) at a new home site in a new community in the southwest part of town on Sunday. The idea, I suppose, was that the dogs would act as a loss leader for those browsing the red-hot real estate market of the last few years of the Twentieth Century. Just looking—and then all of a sudden you've signed away $400,000 and the next thirty years of your life, but you've got a really swell puppy to show for your trouble.

It so happens that my wife and I had already purchased a new home, but were in the market for a dog. Maybe, being fairly new in town, we were a little lonely and needed something else to toss around other than each other. (In the late Sixties when I was living alone in an apartment on West 55th Street in Manhattan, a door-to-door encyclopedia salesman happened to catch me at a vulnerable moment and it seemed eminently logical to me to spend $600 on a Britannica whose sole purpose would be to alleviate my extremely depressing girlfriendless weekend evenings.

Of course, it did no such thing and for the next twenty years I lugged it back and forth across the country while it became more and more outdated and useless. I told myself that I needed it just in case someday I had to draw an accurate picture of a giraffe or, maybe, Napoleon.)

We arrived for the giveaway at about noon and were directed to walk through several model houses in order to get to the dogs. There was a 2200 square-foot one that was attractive and spectacularly appointed with some excellent upgrades and a pool (with waterfall), but we were no rubes and quickly marched forward to our appointment with destiny.

There were a lot of dogs in need of homes, from cute little spaniel puppies to a snarling pit bull with some ugly open wounds from a recent encounter with God-knows-what. Kelli, my wife, delved hip-deep into the fray, while I held back, coolly observing from my post near a saguaro cactus that had been transplanted at a dangerous angle to a swing set. Nearby sat a small orangey-white-haired dog with a very pretty face, but with legs that were way too short for his body. This disproportion made him a bit odd-looking and people were pretty much ignoring him. On the way out of the model I had overheard someone saying that "you have got to see this hilarious freak-dog out back."

He was funny, that was true, but he had a great face. Kelli came back from her survey and said that she hadn't seen anything interesting, to which I replied, "What about this one?" She hadn't even noticed him. Stumpy legs and all. Freak-dog. So she got down on her knees and took a good look and that was it.

The ASPCA people told us he was a golden retriever/basset hound mix and about half a year old. We handed over the $40 licensing and rabies shot fee (free dogs, my ass!) and then helped him into the car, his legs being too short to box with God or, apparently, to enter a Saturn under his own steam. After a stop at the local Target for the requisite canine accoutrements, we headed home.

Kelli named him Misha after Mikhail Baryshnikov, whose nickname is Misha, after the ballet-like turnout of his front paws. I wanted to call him Stumpy, but that idea was shot down. We could as well have named him Sneezy or Snotty, because that's pretty much all he did for the next two weeks. It turns out that when we got him he had a bad case of what's called kennel cough, the chief symptom of which is a lot of very aggressive and violent sneezing which sends the head into a forty-five degree spin rocketing reams of juicy mucus across the floor and four or five feet up the nearest wall.

These outbursts notwithstanding, Misha was quiet as a mouse. Not a whimper, bark or howl at the moon escaped his countenance. A mute dog. Interesting. And not a bad deal, either, because who in their right mind wants some yappy little bastard out in the back yard at all hours of the day and night? We didn't feel the need for a watchdog and I wasn't about to try teaching him to "Speak!" anyway. So, a nice low-key pooch—what could be better?

We proceeded to nurse him back to health and the sneezes eventually disappeared and the better he felt, the more playful he got, but always a quiet, thoughtful playfulness. We loved him and took delight in our silent new companion, and then we took him out for a ride one day and as we were backing out of the garage a neighbor was walking by and got a little closer to the car perhaps than he, from a dog's point of view, should have been and Misha let out a bark. It was a giant, building-rattler of a bark, which, in the confines of our little car, had the sonic force of a vast new Mount St. Helen's eruption. A sudden unexpected explosion in the back seat about a foot from my right ear. I thought I had perhaps knocked the garage off its foundation and briefly considered having a heart attack.

And so that's the story of how we got a dog and how he became normal, and then one day he took us both aside and told us that it was too damn hot for a dog to be hanging out in the desert in Las Vegas and how we might consider, for his sake, moving to a slightly more hospitable climate, a place not unlike where I'm writing this introduction right now, where there's plenty of snow in which to romp in the winter and plenty of moths for a dog to catch in the summer.

—Jack Ziegler, Sharon, CT, 2006

"Seven-thirty! Dinner is late!! I'm furious!! _Stop that wagging!!!_"

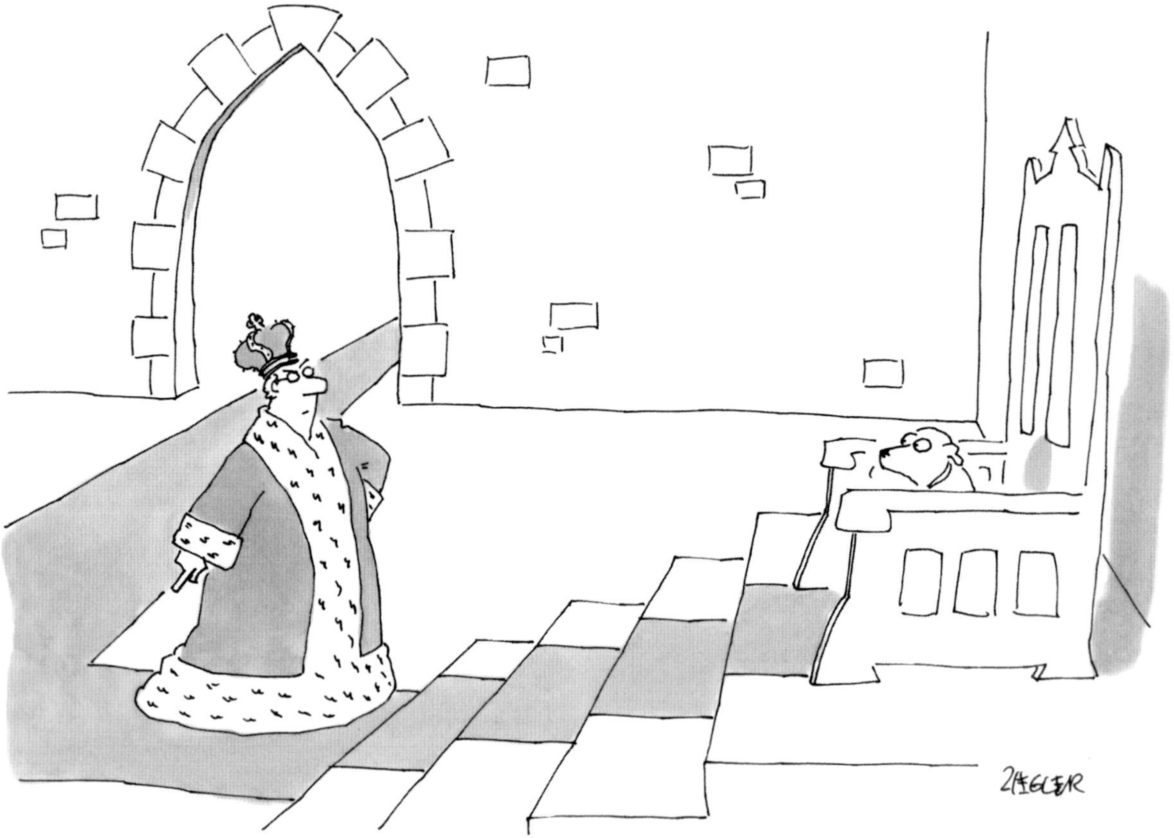
ZIEGLER

"I met him only once. It was at a church picnic. But before I knew it—whammo!—puppies."

"Sparky, you're the best damn biscuit salesman we've ever had, but I need you to stop chasing after the cats down in accounting."

"I was into Zen for a while, too, but then I discovered the rawhide chew."

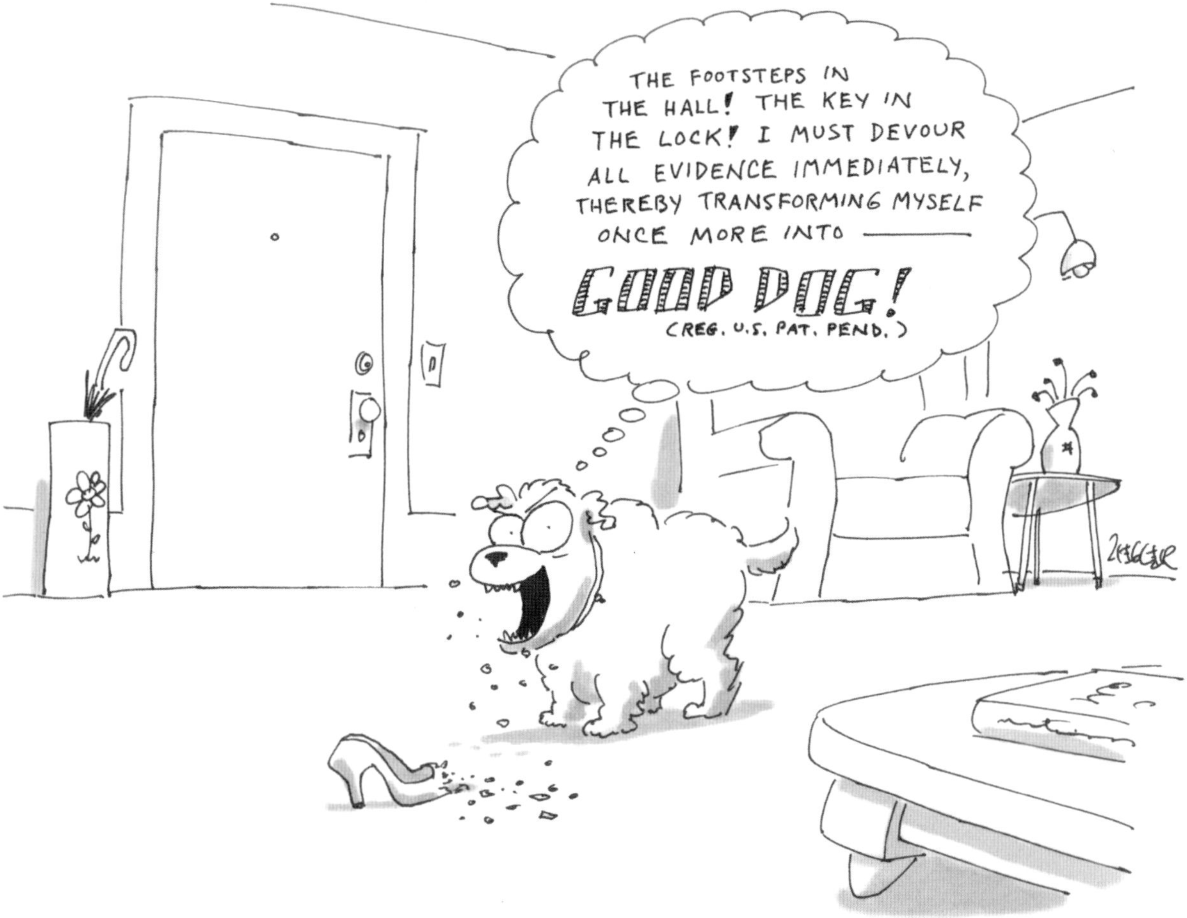
THE FOOTSTEPS IN THE HALL! THE KEY IN THE LOCK! I MUST DEVOUR ALL EVIDENCE IMMEDIATELY, THEREBY TRANSFORMING MYSELF ONCE MORE INTO ——
GOOD DOG!
(REG. U.S. PAT. PEND.)

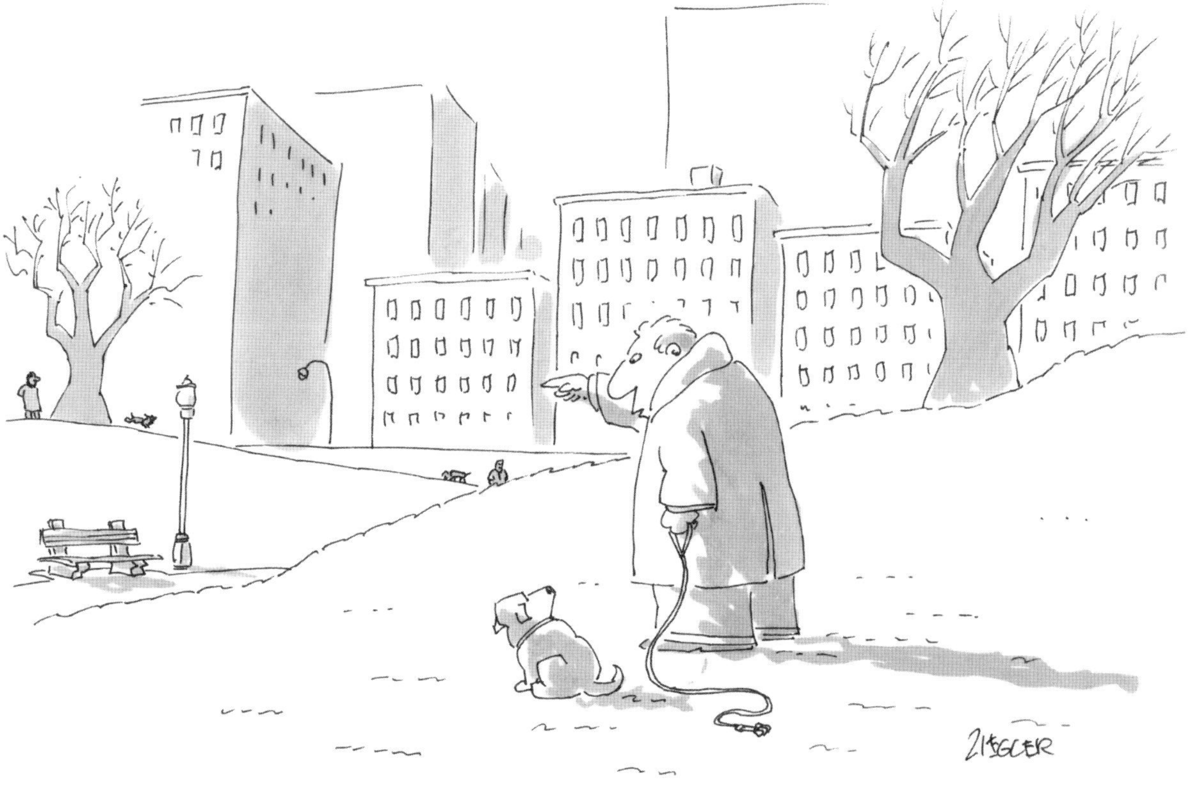
ZIEGLER

"Let the bells of freedom ring. But only for five minutes, O.K.?"

"I adore Sundays—getting to sleep for twenty-three hours, instead of twenty-two."

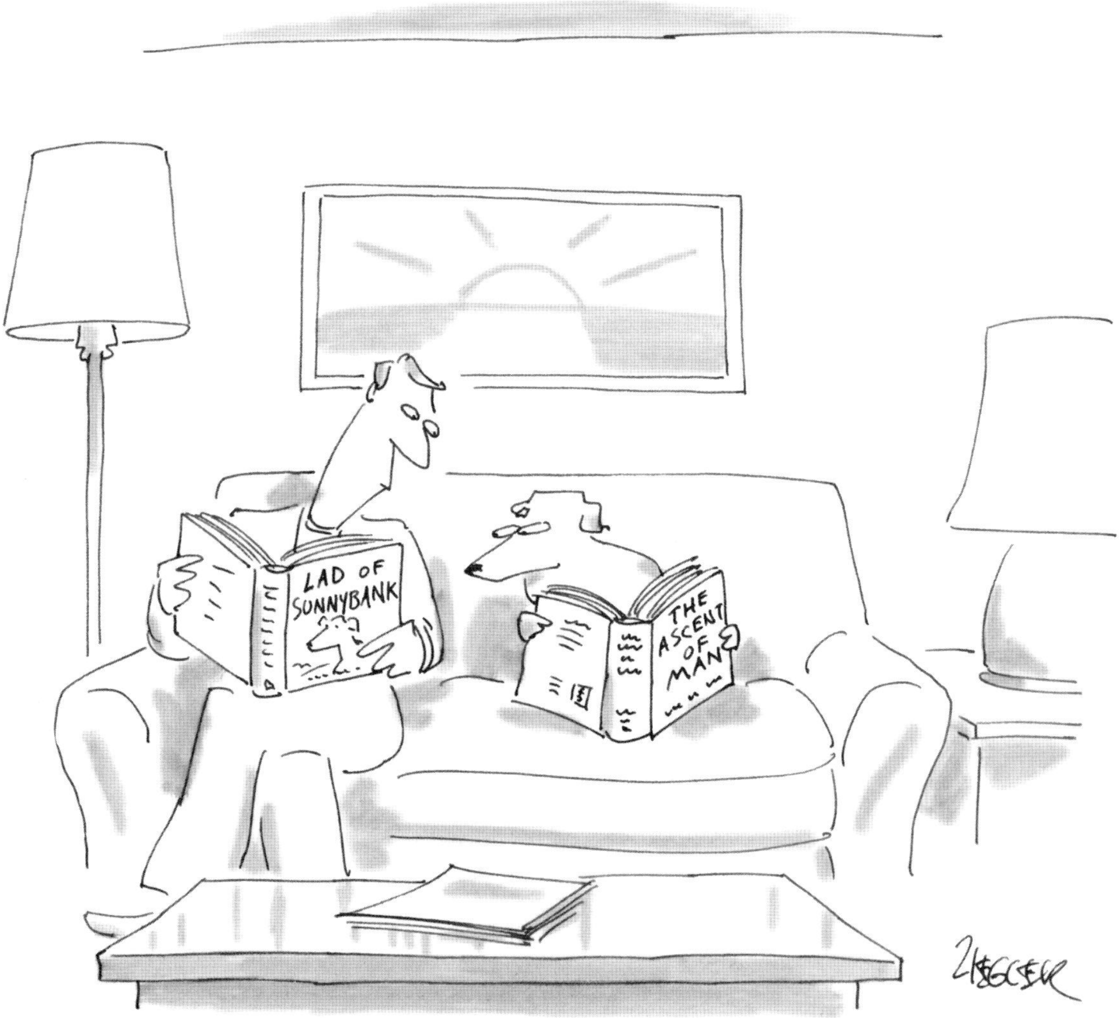
LAD OF SUNNYBANK
THE ASCENT OF MAN

"And it will be more pleasant for all of us if, for once in your life, you don't kiss anyone hello."

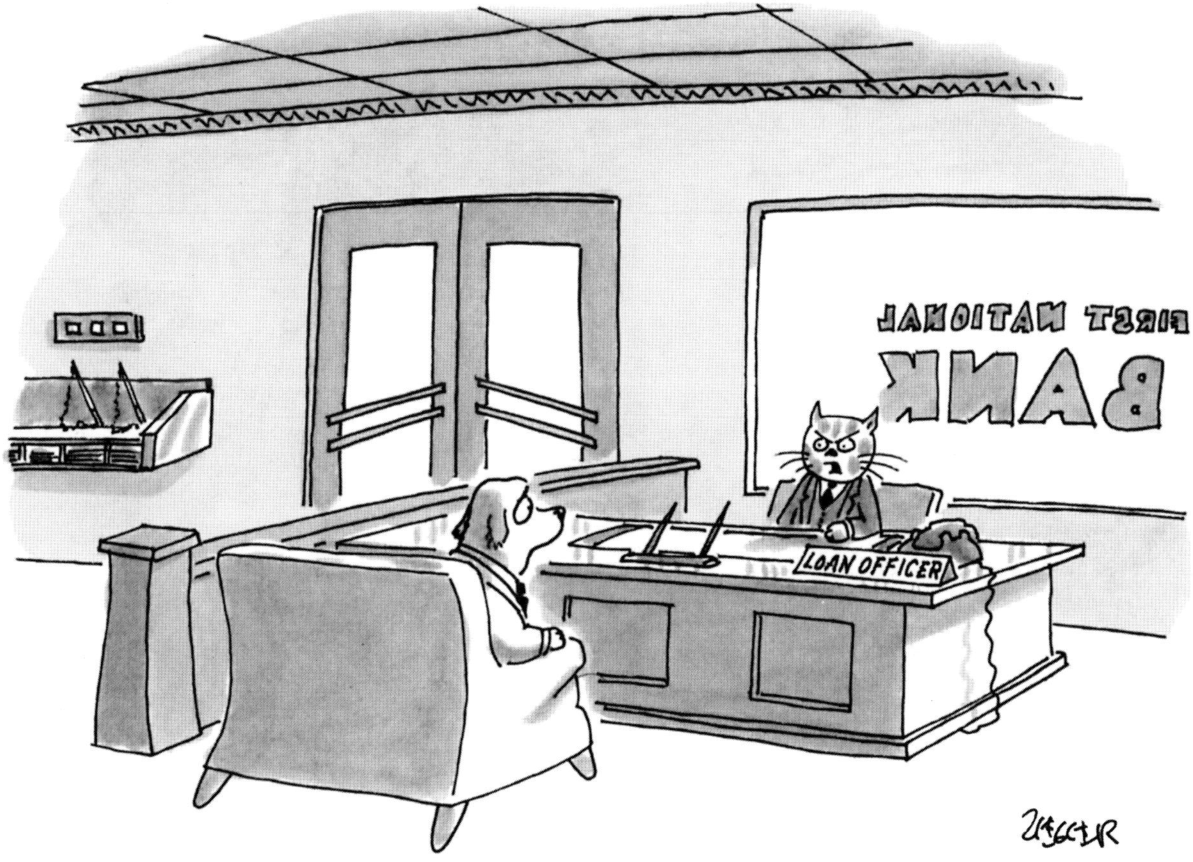
FIRST NATIONAL
BANK
LOAN OFFICER

"Beg."

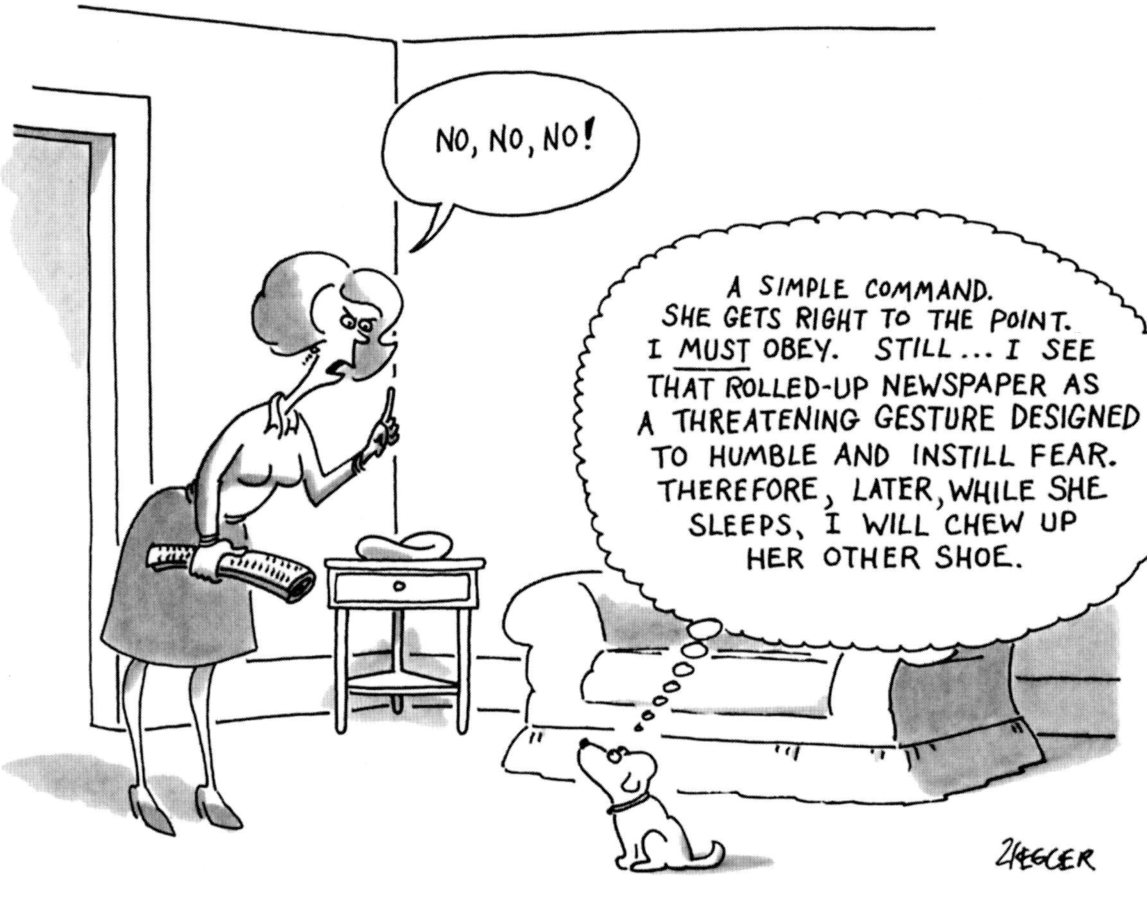
NO, NO, NO!
A SIMPLE COMMAND. SHE GETS RIGHT TO THE POINT. I MUST OBEY. STILL... I SEE THAT ROLLED-UP NEWSPAPER AS A THREATENING GESTURE DESIGNED TO HUMBLE AND INSTILL FEAR. THEREFORE, LATER, WHILE SHE SLEEPS, I WILL CHEW UP HER OTHER SHOE.
ZIEGLER

"It's a cat calendar, so it may not be all that accurate."

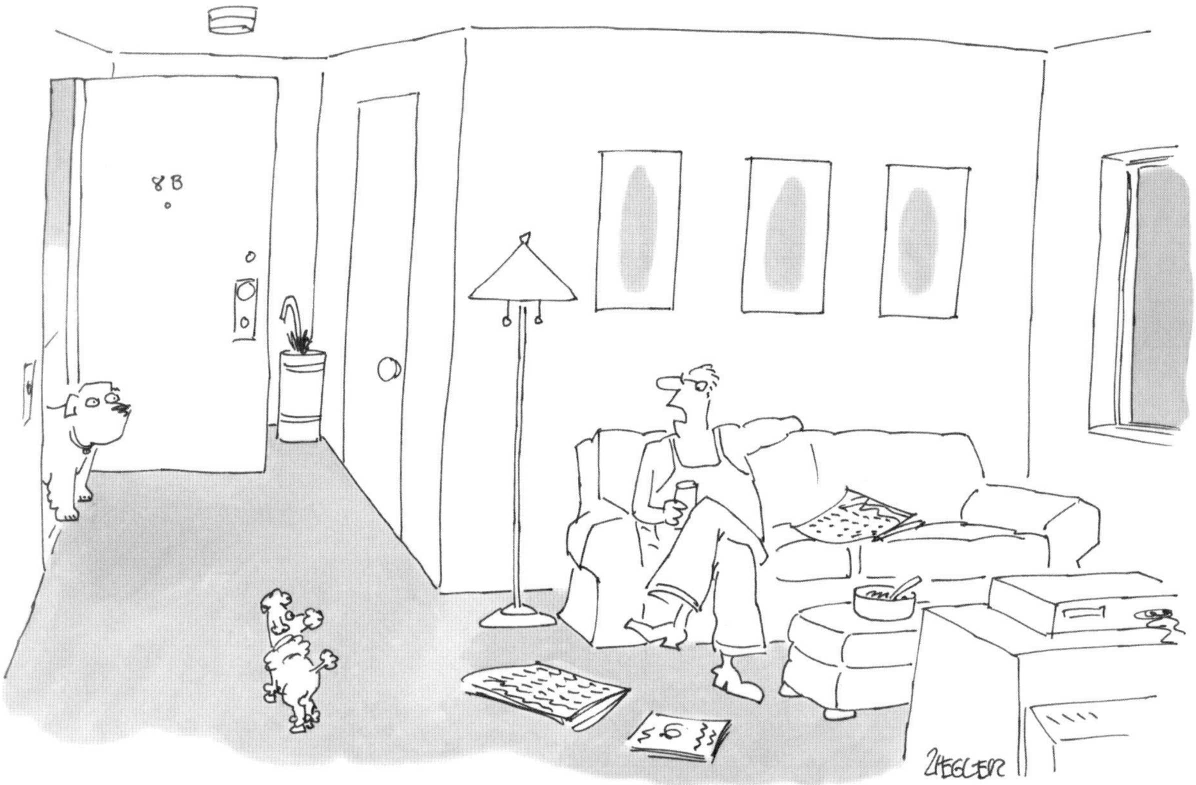
8B
ZIEGLER

"Hey, Romeo! Just have her back by eleven!"

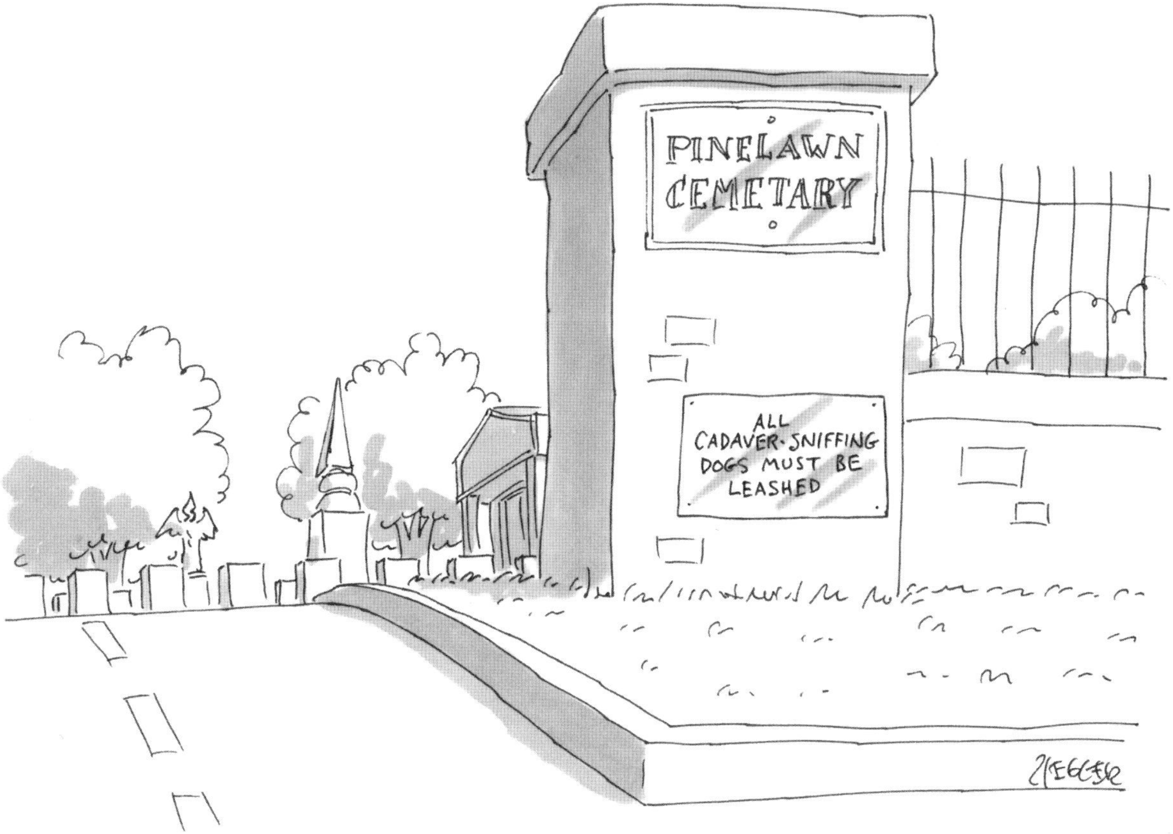
PINELAWN CEMETARY
ALL CADAVER-SNIFFING DOGS MUST BE LEASHED
ZIEGLER

"Hey! Did it ever occur to you that someone might want to stop and smell the parking meters?"

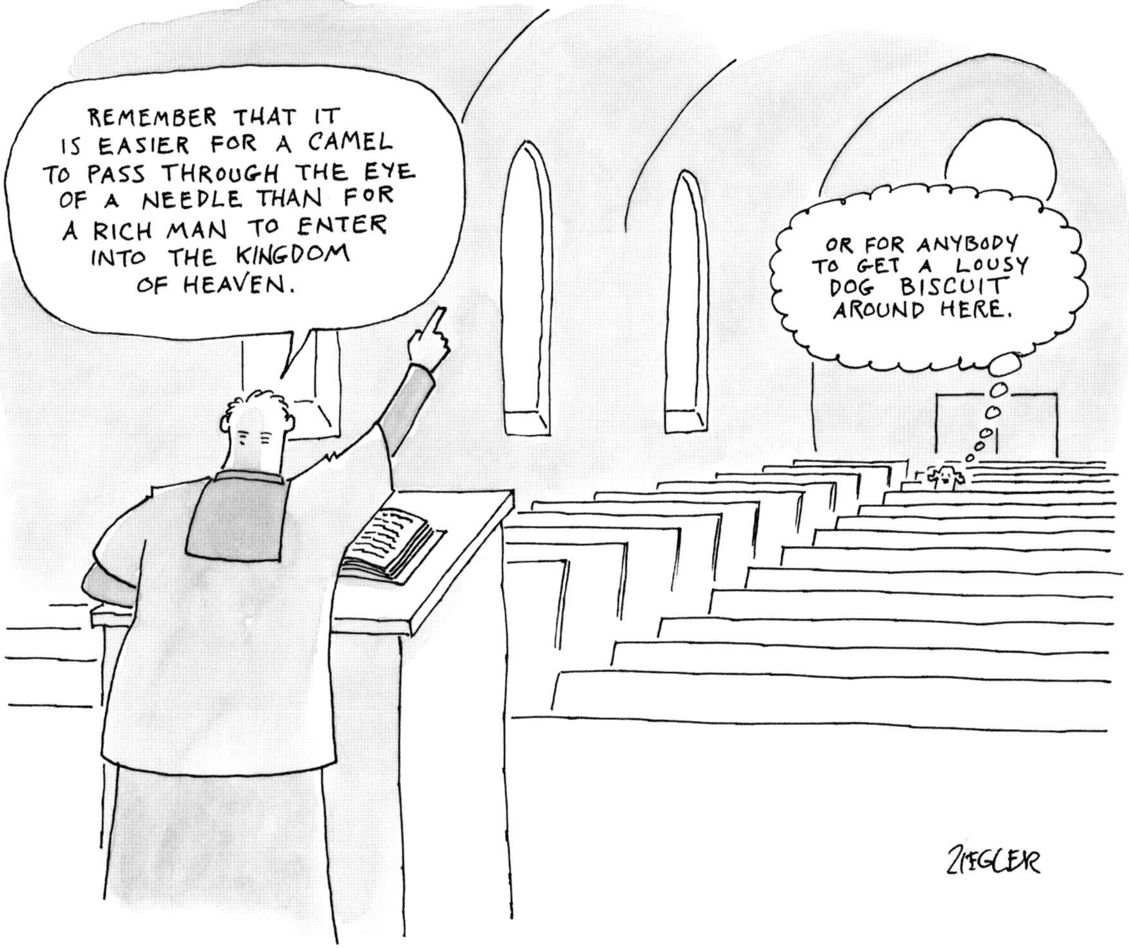
REMEMBER THAT IT IS EASIER FOR A CAMEL TO PASS THROUGH THE EYE OF A NEEDLE THAN FOR A RICH MAN TO ENTER INTO THE KINGDOM OF HEAVEN.
OR FOR ANYBODY TO GET A LOUSY DOG BISCUIT AROUND HERE.
ZIEGLER

"*Your best friend also seems to be enjoying your refusal to ask for directions.*"

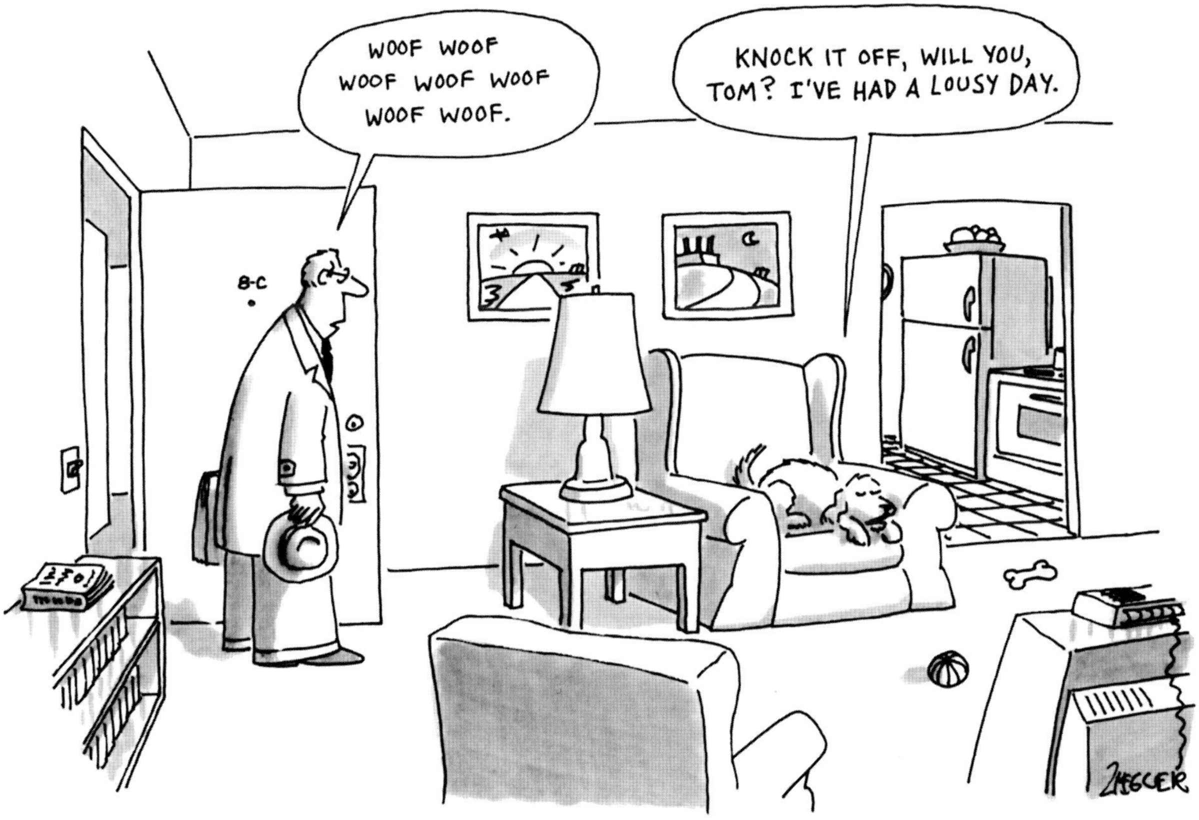
WOOF WOOF WOOF WOOF WOOF WOOF WOOF.
KNOCK IT OFF, WILL YOU, TOM? I'VE HAD A LOUSY DAY.
8-C

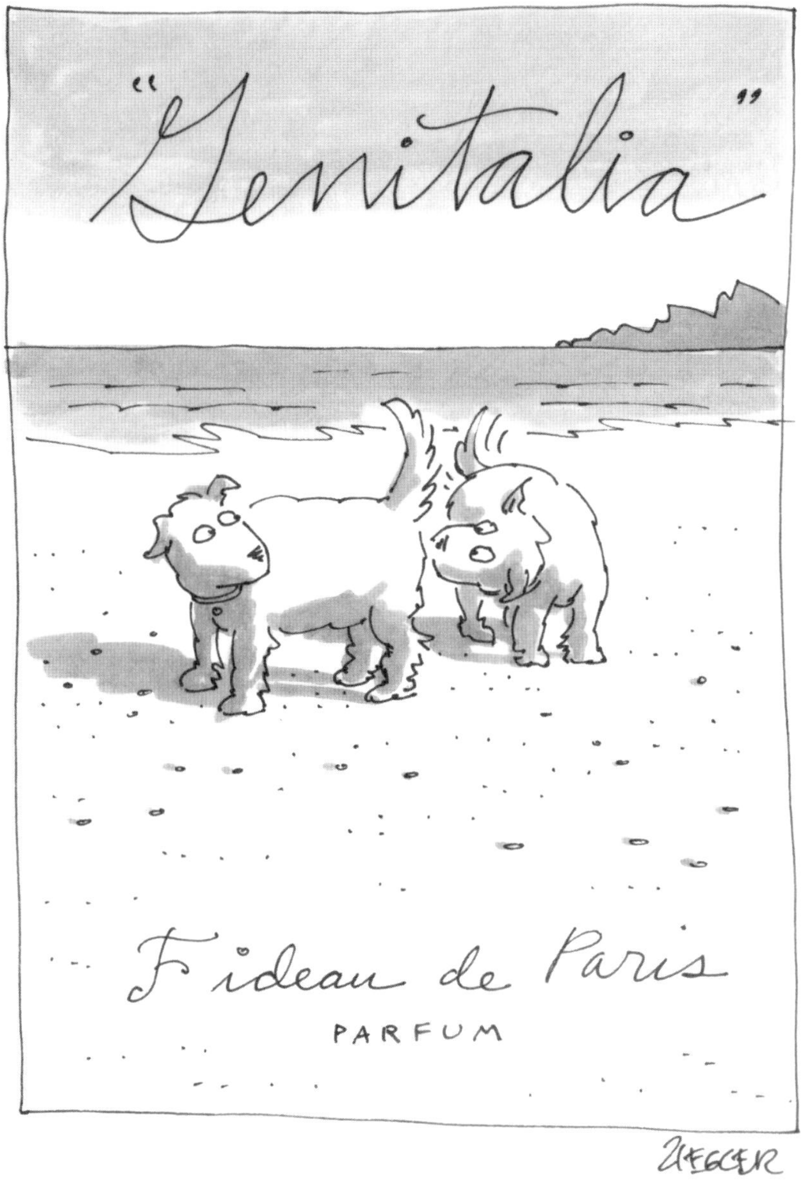
"Genitalia"
Fideau de Paris
PARFUM
ZIEGLER

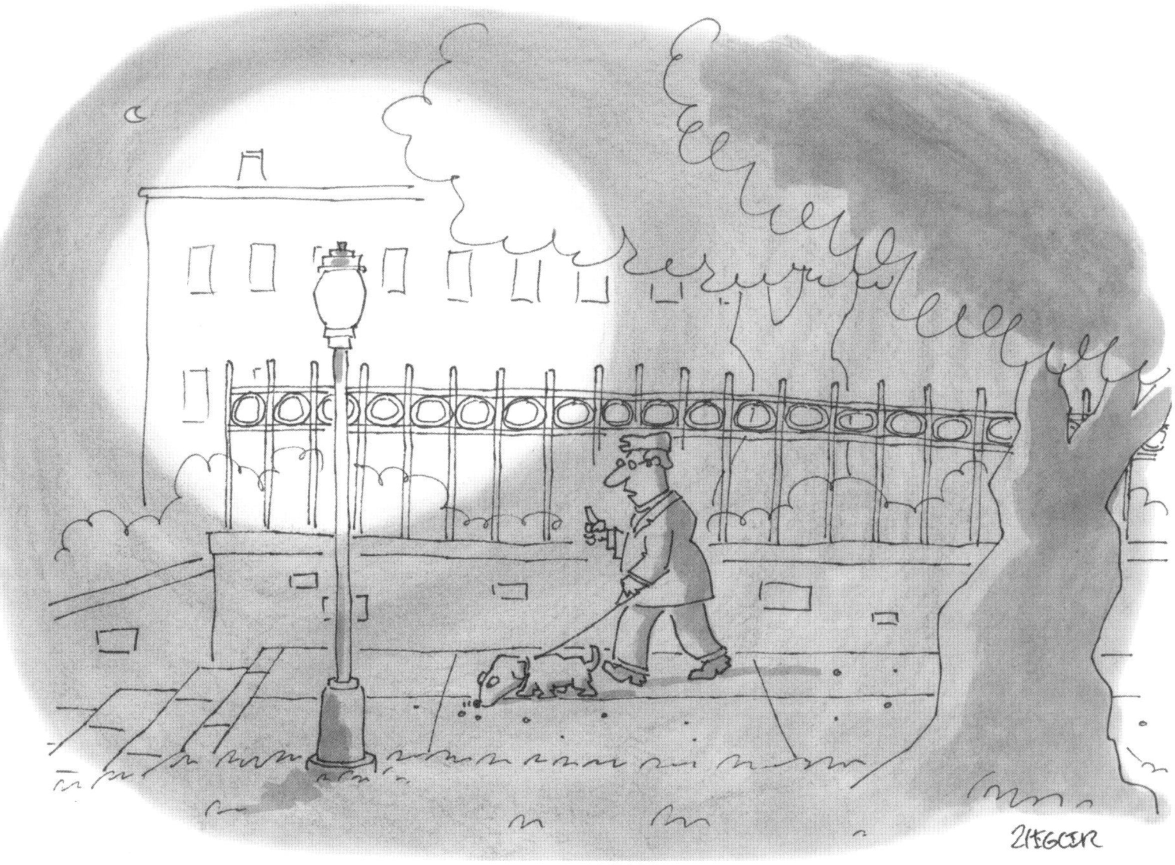
ZIEGLER

"O.K., this next one I'm going to hum is from an old Miles Davis LP. You tell me the name of the song and also which album it's from."

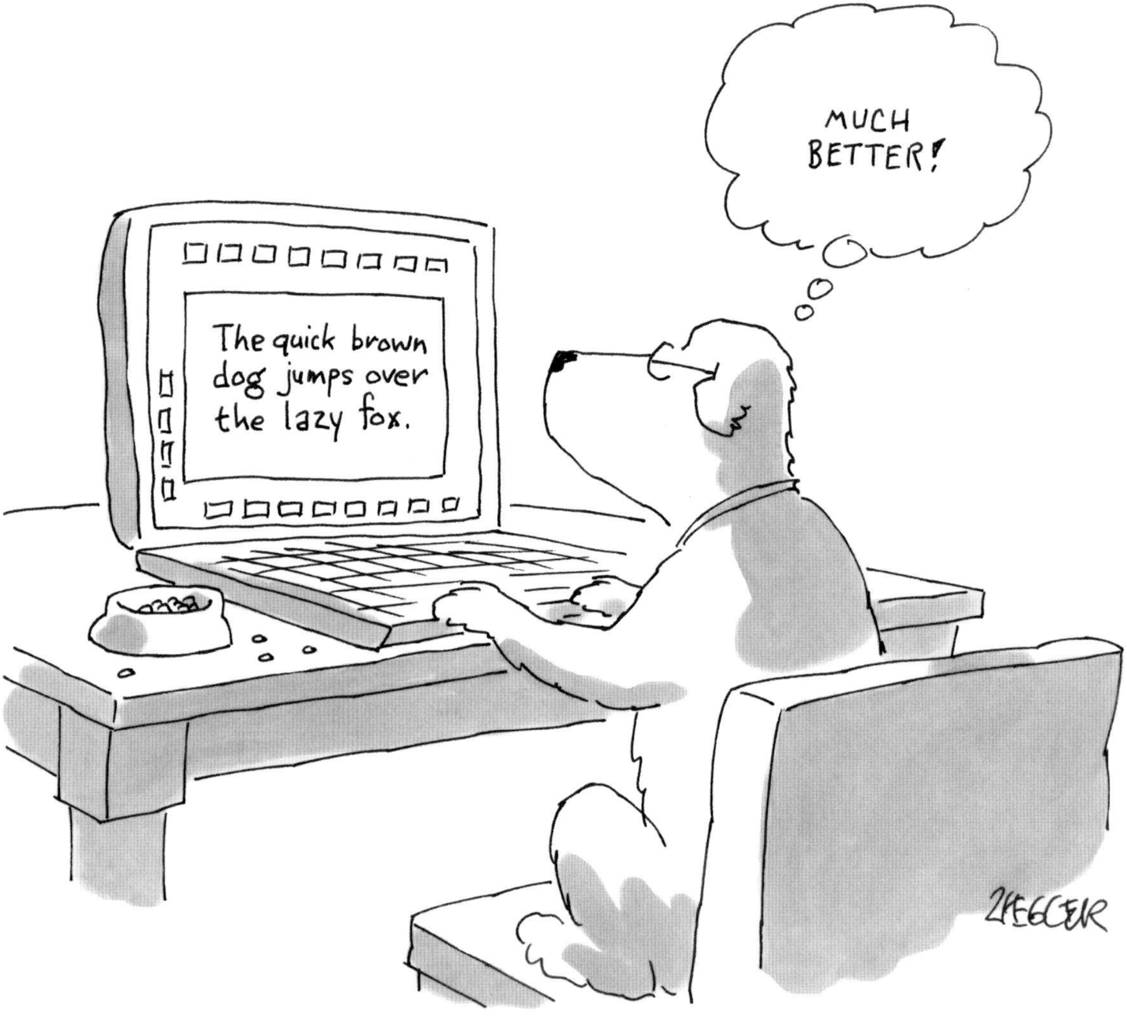
MUCH BETTER!
The quick brown dog jumps over the lazy fox.
ZIEGLER

SAMSON AND HIS DOG, HERCULES

33

"Here's a cute little human-interest item—oh, never mind."

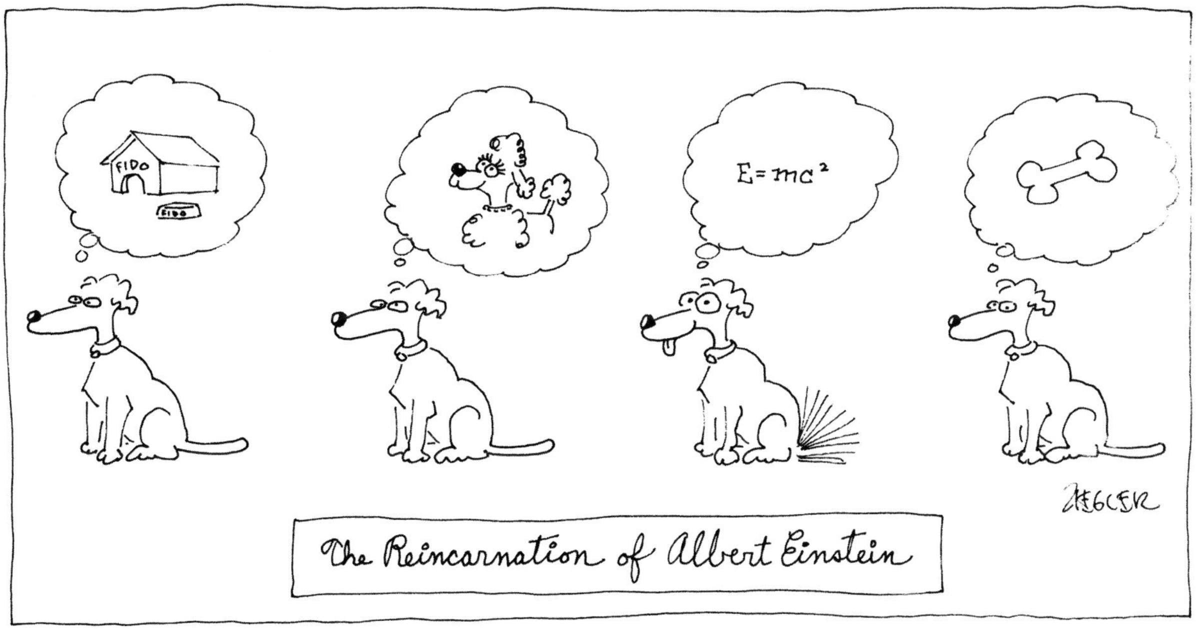
FIDO
FIDO
E = mc²
ZIEGLER
The Reincarnation of Albert Einstein

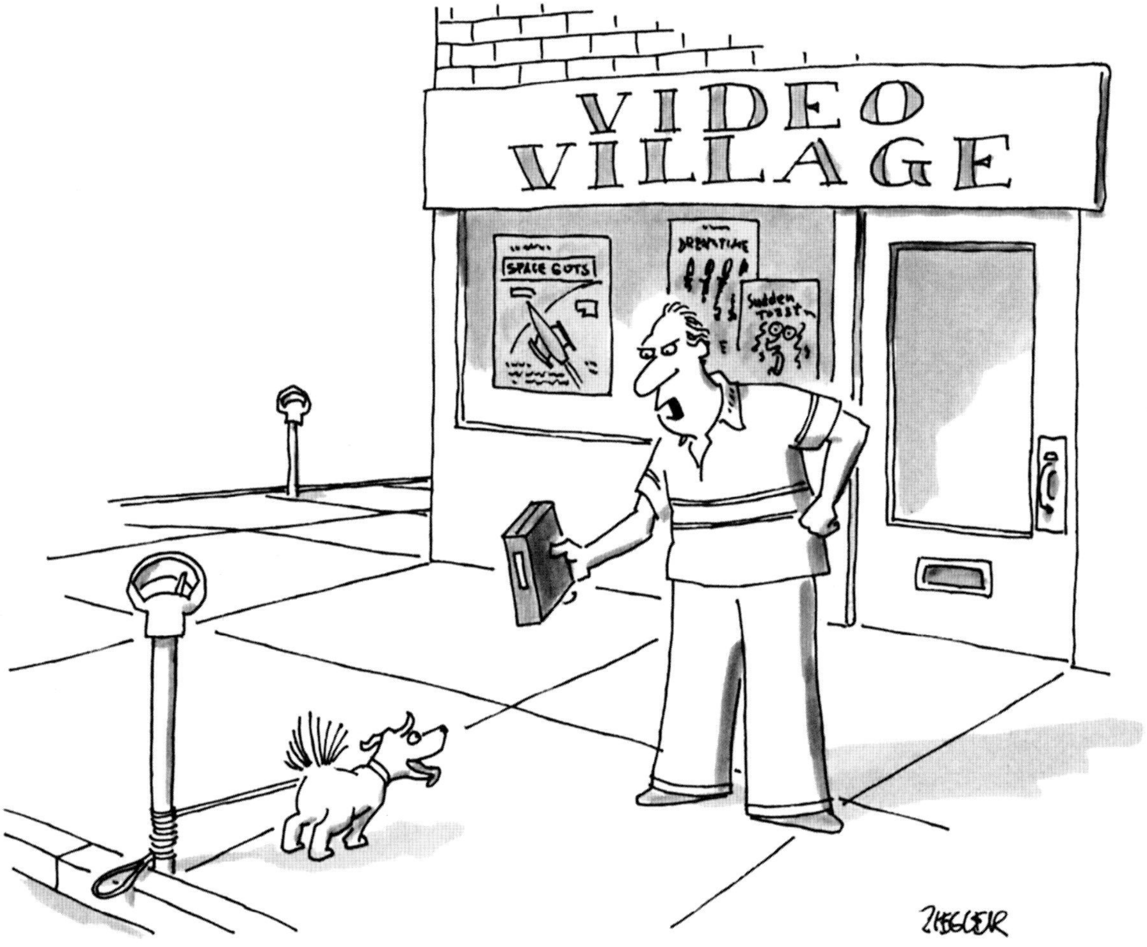
VIDEO VILLAGE
SPACE GUTS
DREAMTIME
Sudden Toast

"O.K., O.K., here's 'Lassie, Come Home' again! <u>Now</u> are you happy?"

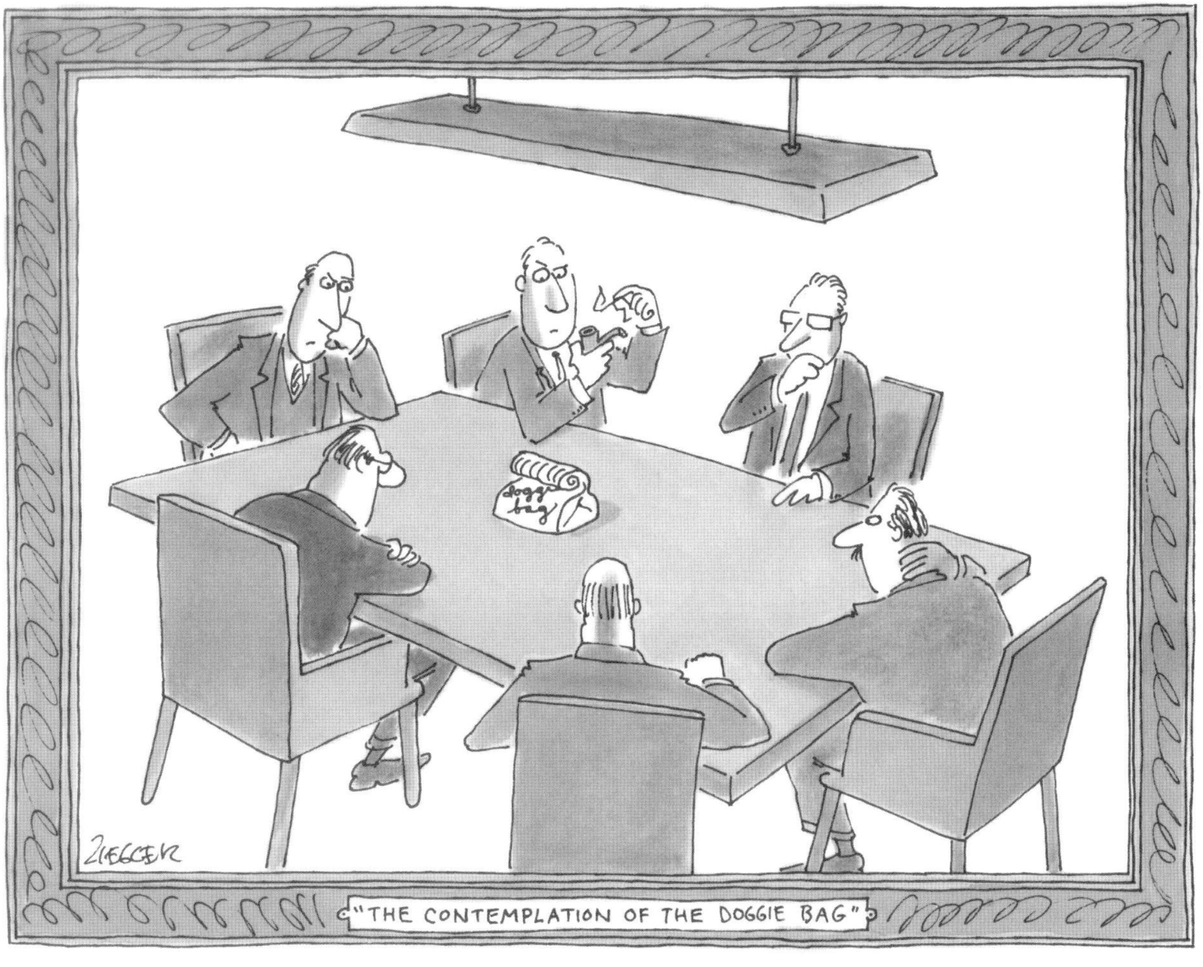
doggie bag
ZIEGLER
"THE CONTEMPLATION OF THE DOGGIE BAG"

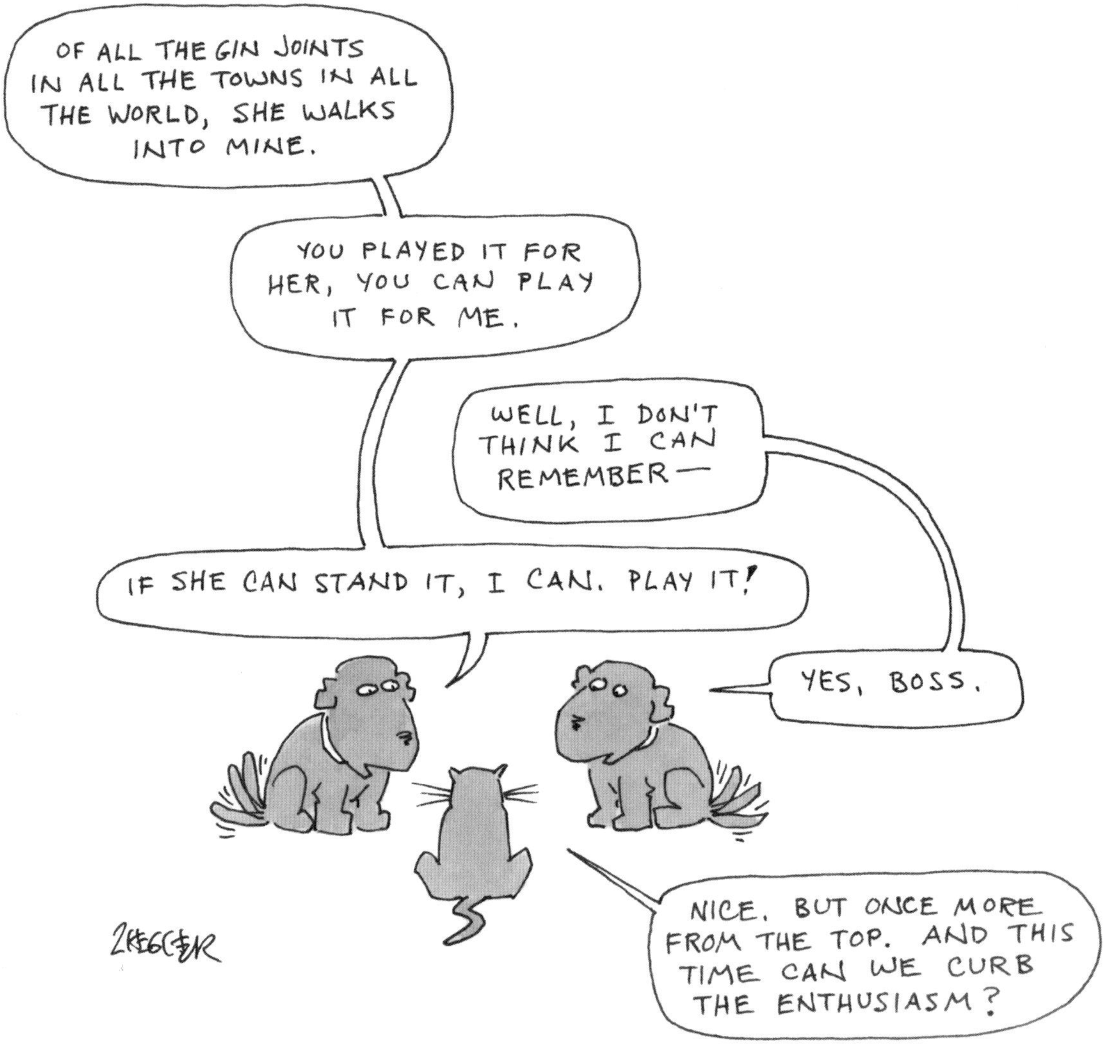
OF ALL THE GIN JOINTS IN ALL THE TOWNS IN ALL THE WORLD, SHE WALKS INTO MINE.
YOU PLAYED IT FOR HER, YOU CAN PLAY IT FOR ME.
WELL, I DON'T THINK I CAN REMEMBER—
IF SHE CAN STAND IT, I CAN. PLAY IT!
YES, BOSS.
NICE. BUT ONCE MORE FROM THE TOP. AND THIS TIME CAN WE CURB THE ENTHUSIASM?
ZIEGLER

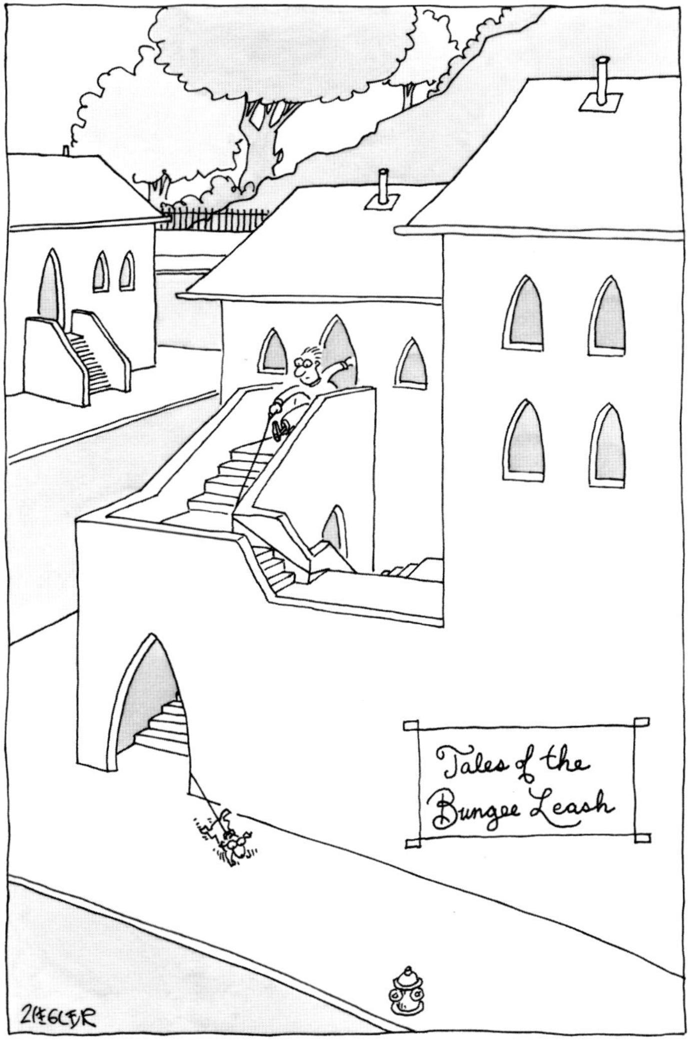
Tales of the Bungee Leash
ZIEGLER

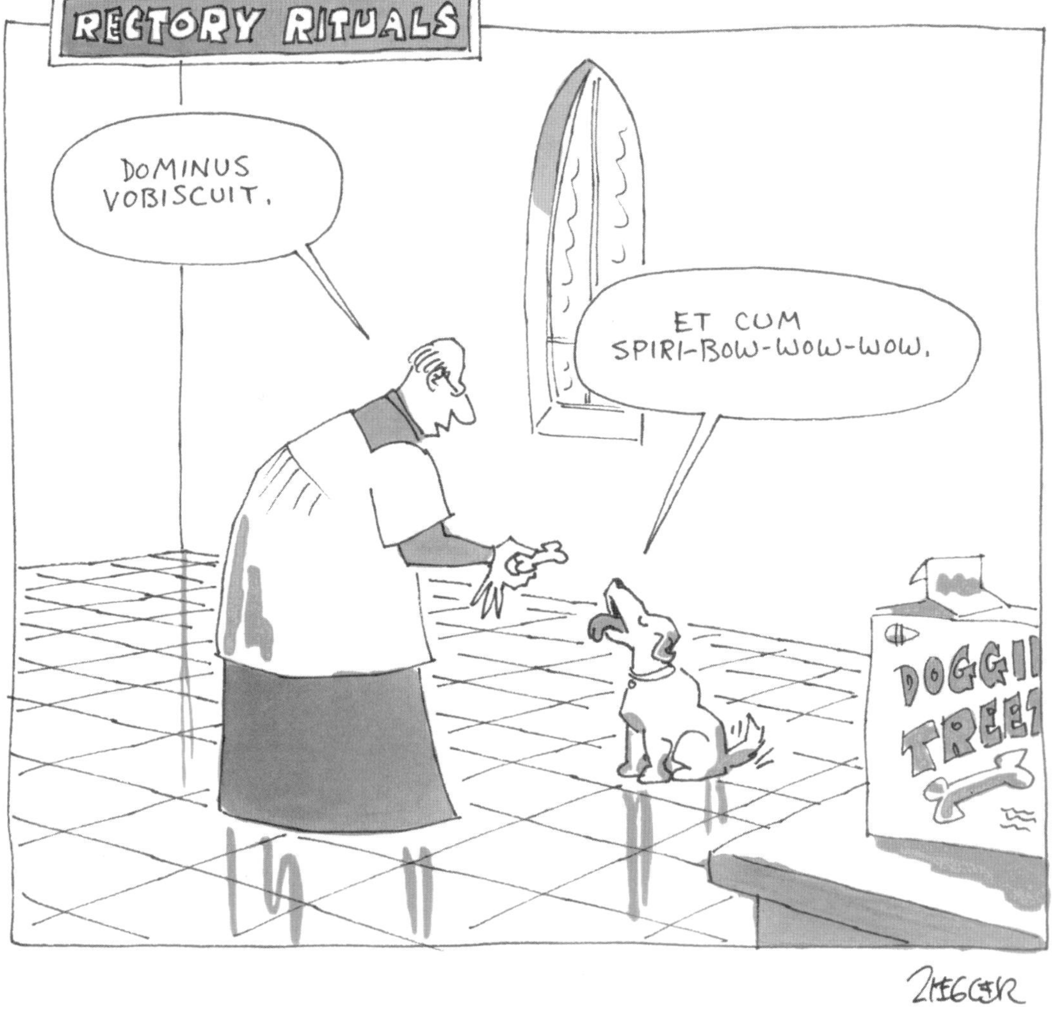
RECTORY RITUALS
DOMINUS VOBISCUIT.
ET CUM SPIRI-BOW-WOW-WOW.
ZIEGLER

SUDDENLY IT HIT ME. THE CEREMONIAL SCENT-LAYINGS IN THE STAIRWELL WERE OVER. THE RITUAL GNAWINGS ON THE LEATHER SOFA — GONE, AND THE SACRED SCATTERING OF MY BELOVED HAIR ALL OVER THE WALL-TO-WALL — ADIOS, AMIGOS....

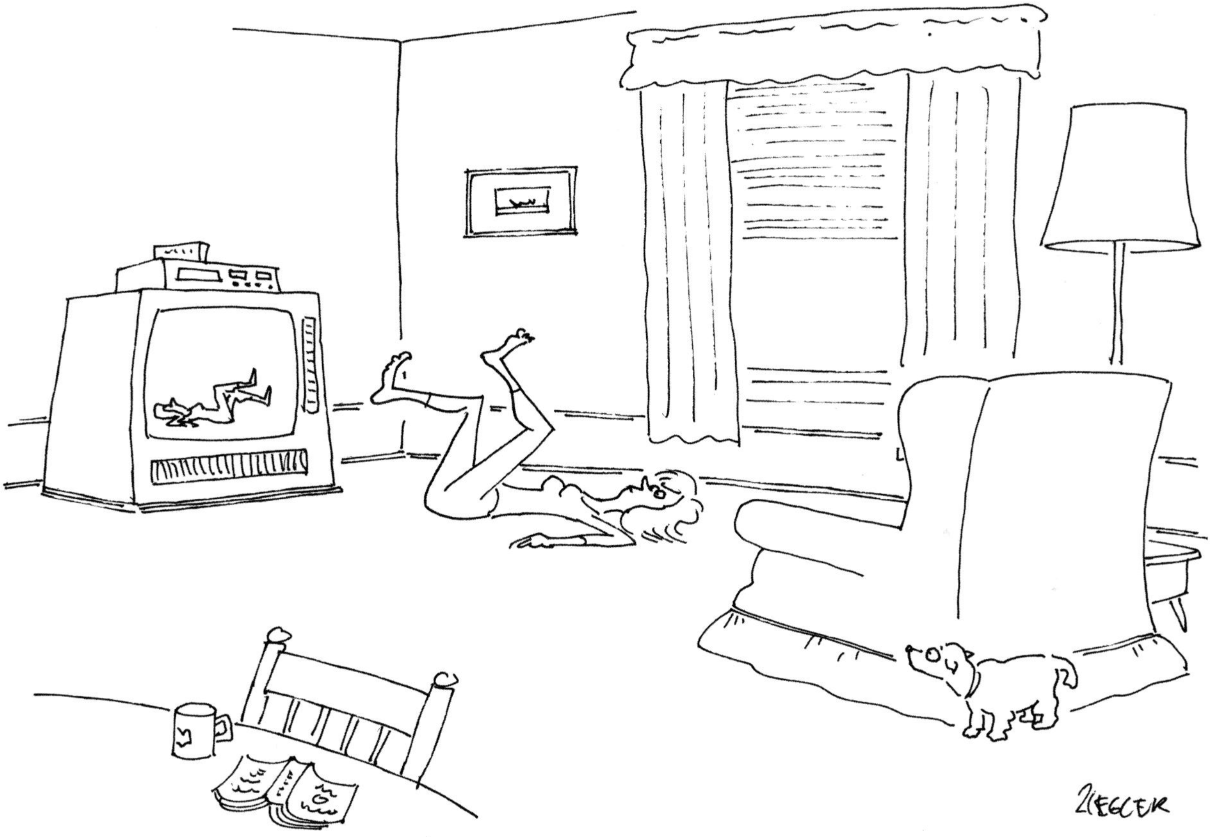
ZIEGLER

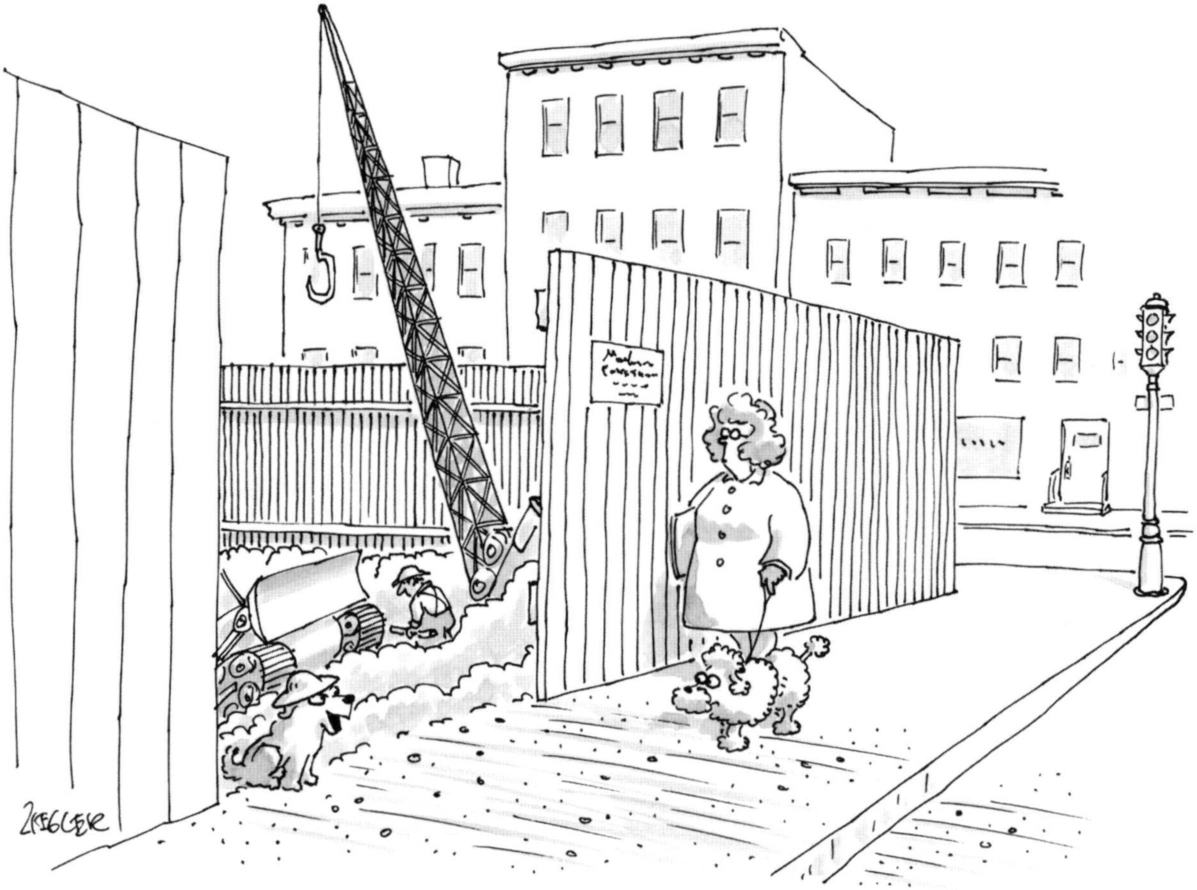
ZIEGLER

*"Hey, baby, what's happenin'? How's about a little kiss, mama?
Woof, woof, woof? Ar–oooooooo!"*

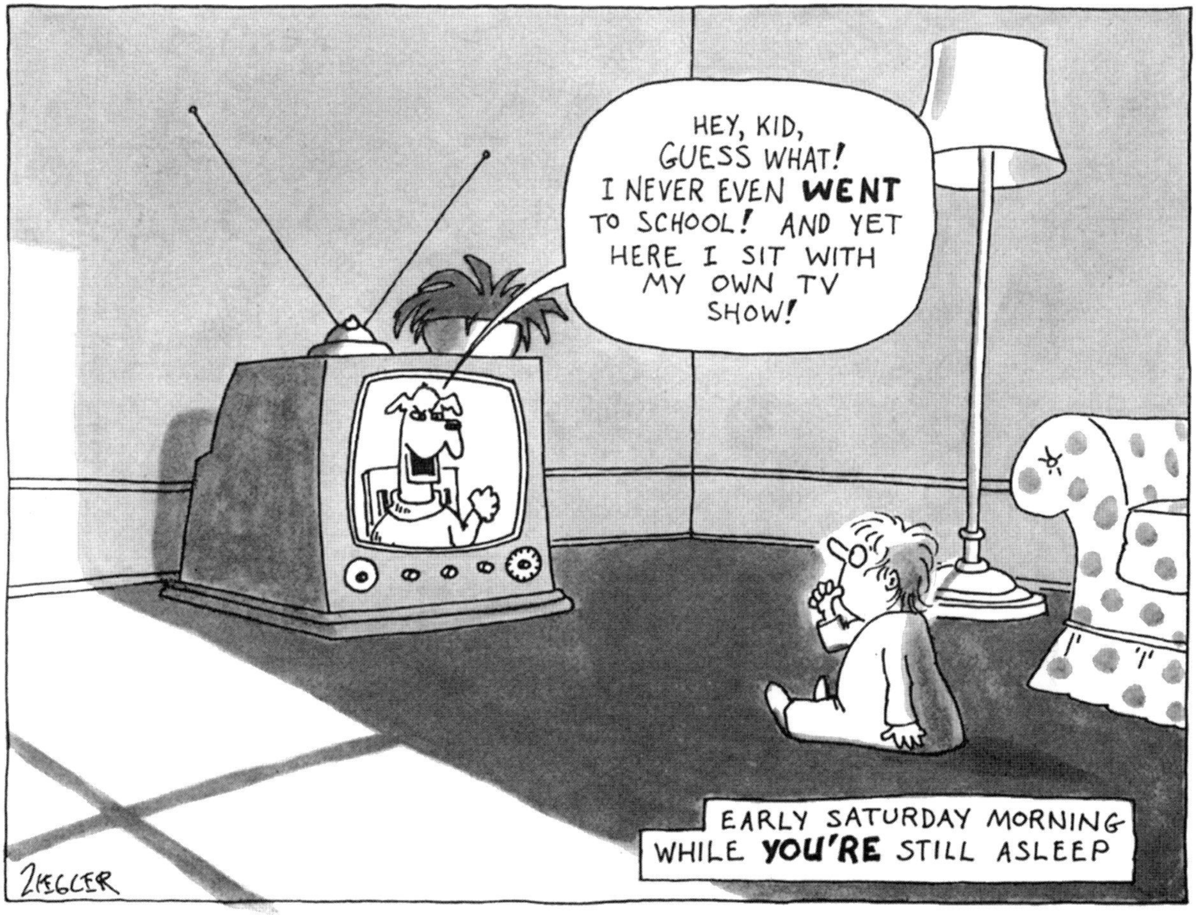
HEY, KID, GUESS WHAT! I NEVER EVEN WENT TO SCHOOL! AND YET HERE I SIT WITH MY OWN TV SHOW!
EARLY SATURDAY MORNING WHILE YOU'RE STILL ASLEEP
ZIEGLER

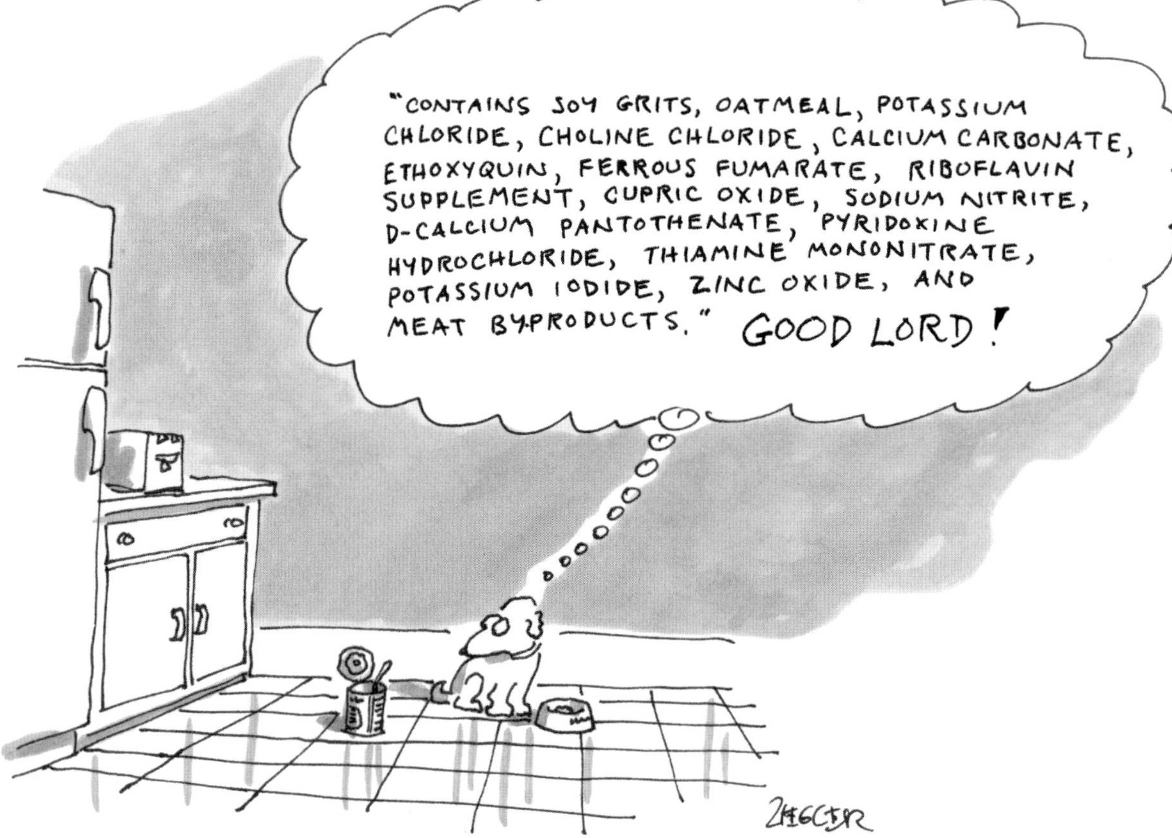
"CONTAINS SOY GRITS, OATMEAL, POTASSIUM CHLORIDE, CHOLINE CHLORIDE, CALCIUM CARBONATE, ETHOXYQUIN, FERROUS FUMARATE, RIBOFLAVIN SUPPLEMENT, CUPRIC OXIDE, SODIUM NITRITE, D-CALCIUM PANTOTHENATE, PYRIDOXINE HYDROCHLORIDE, THIAMINE MONONITRATE, POTASSIUM IODIDE, ZINC OXIDE, AND MEAT BYPRODUCTS." GOOD LORD!
ZIEGLER

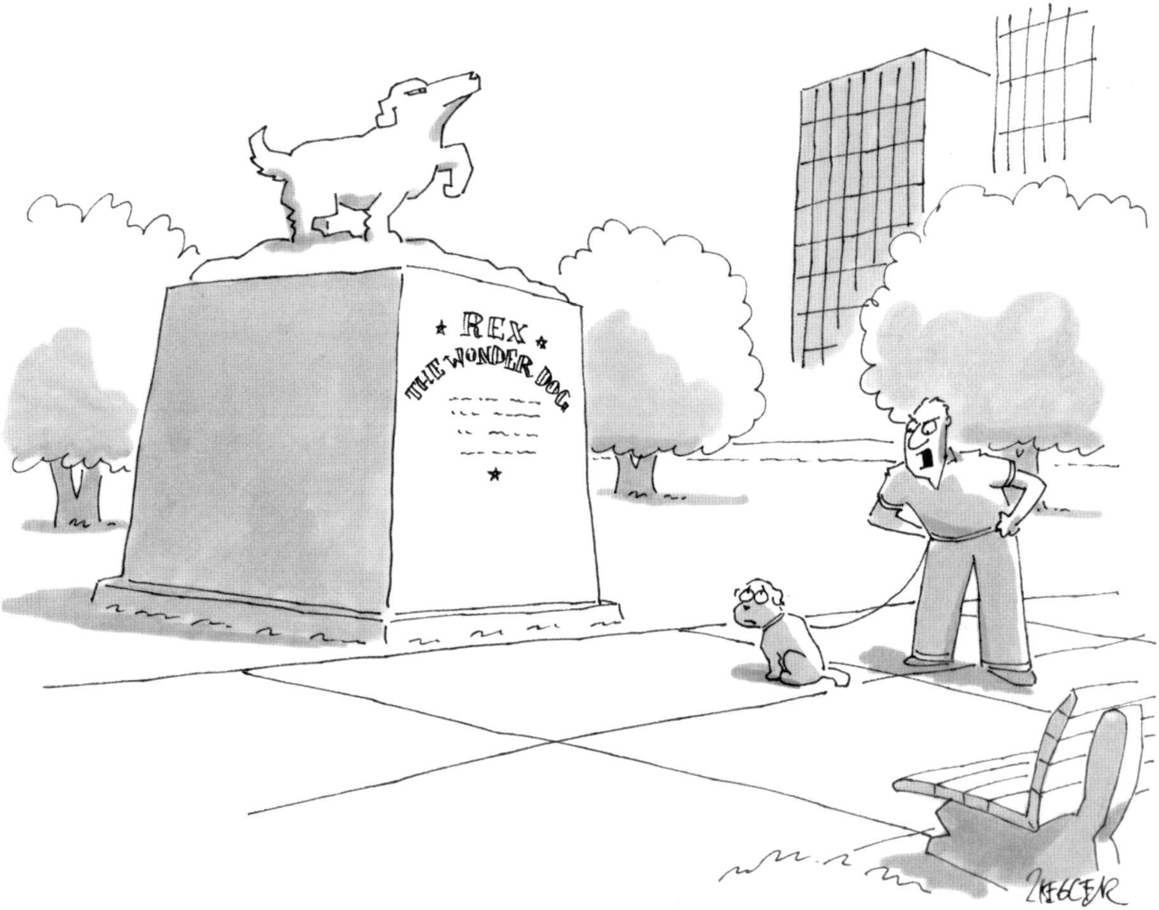
REX
THE WONDER DOG
ZIEGLER

"Imbecile!!"

"They say the dog food here is really good."

TAPE LOOP LAFFS
SIT.
GOOD DOG.
SIT.
GOOD DOG.
SIT.
GOOD DOG.
ZIEGLER

"You haven't a clue what I'm talking about, do you?"

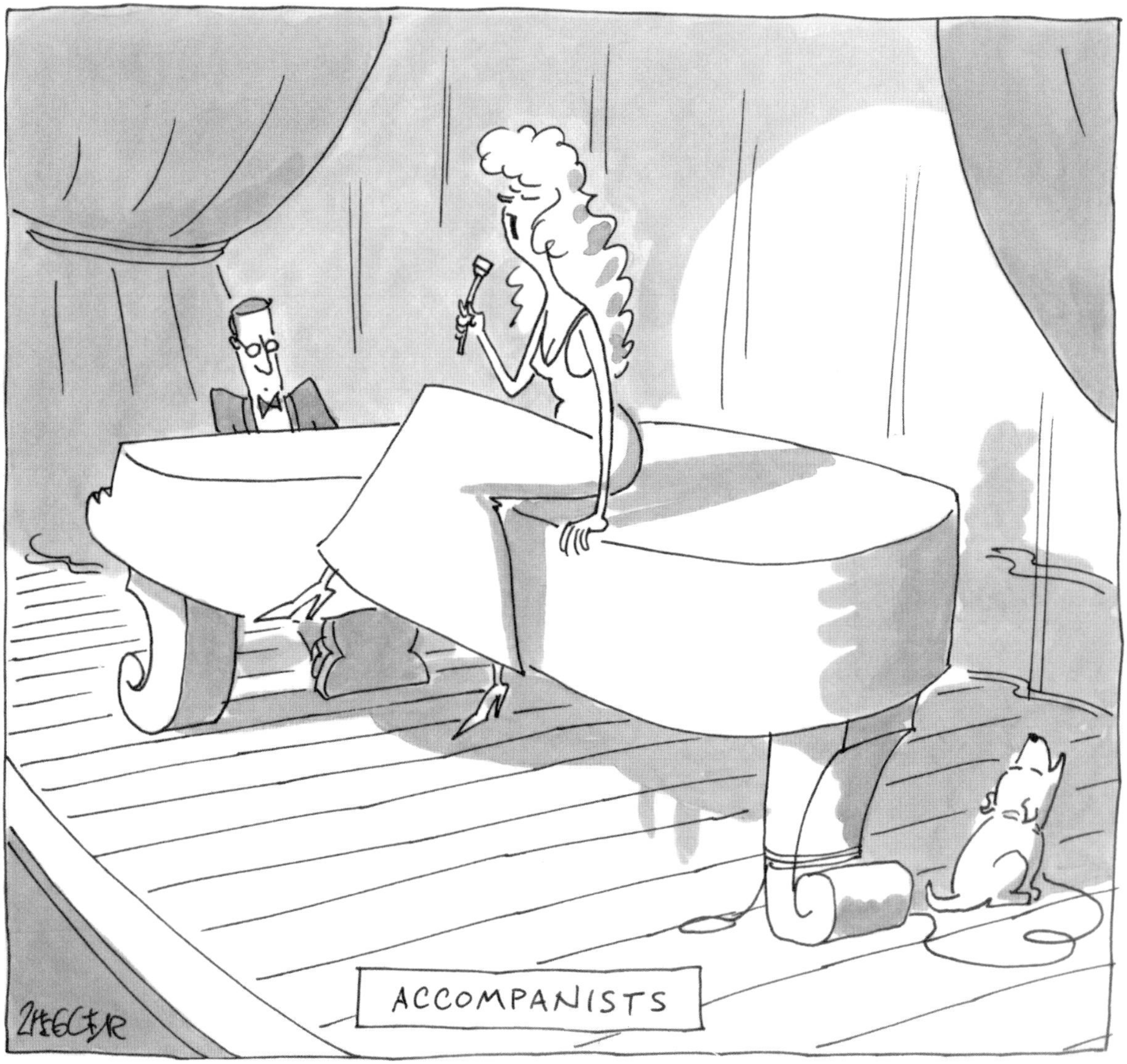
ACCOMPANISTS
ZIEGLER

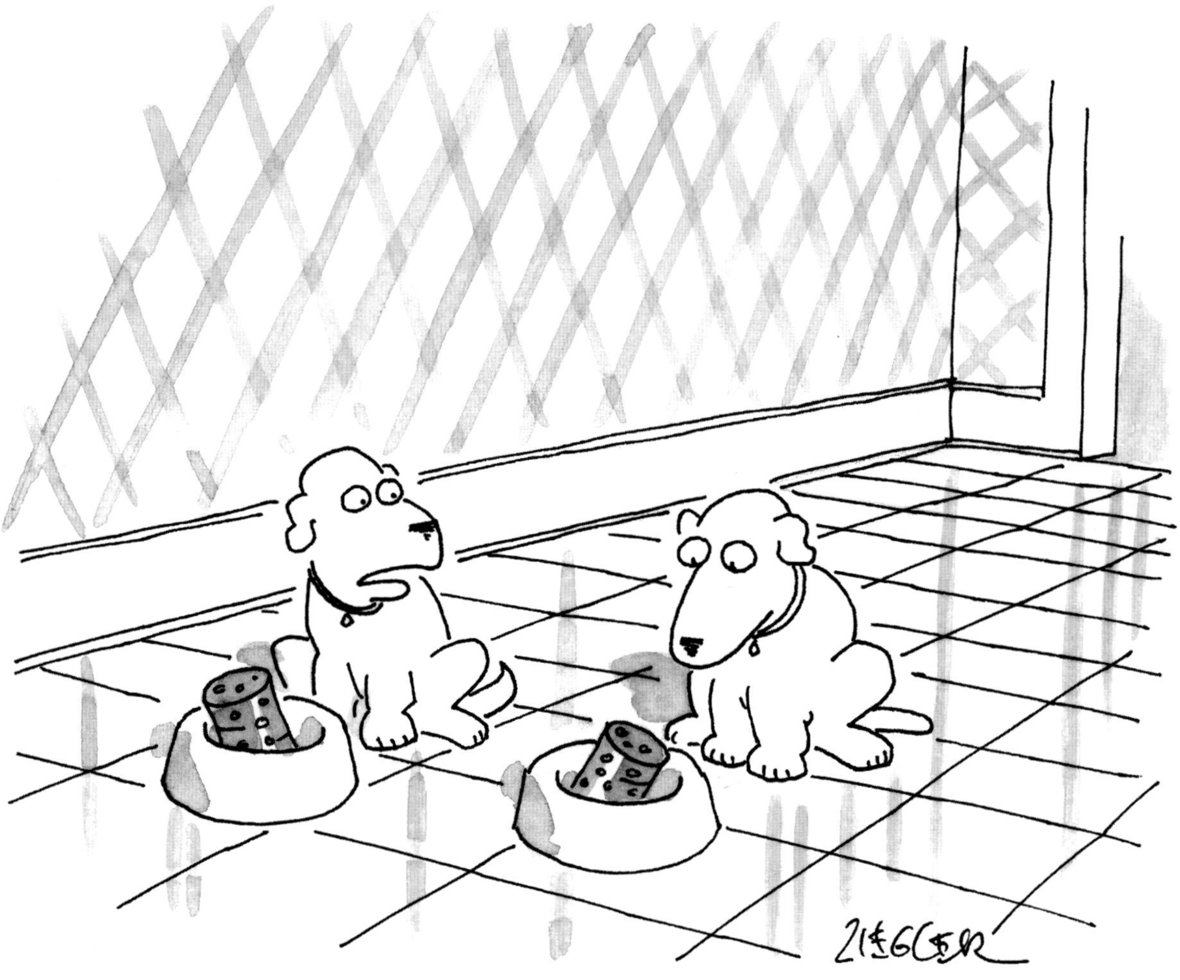
ZIEGLER

"Just keep reminding yourself that canned is better than dry."

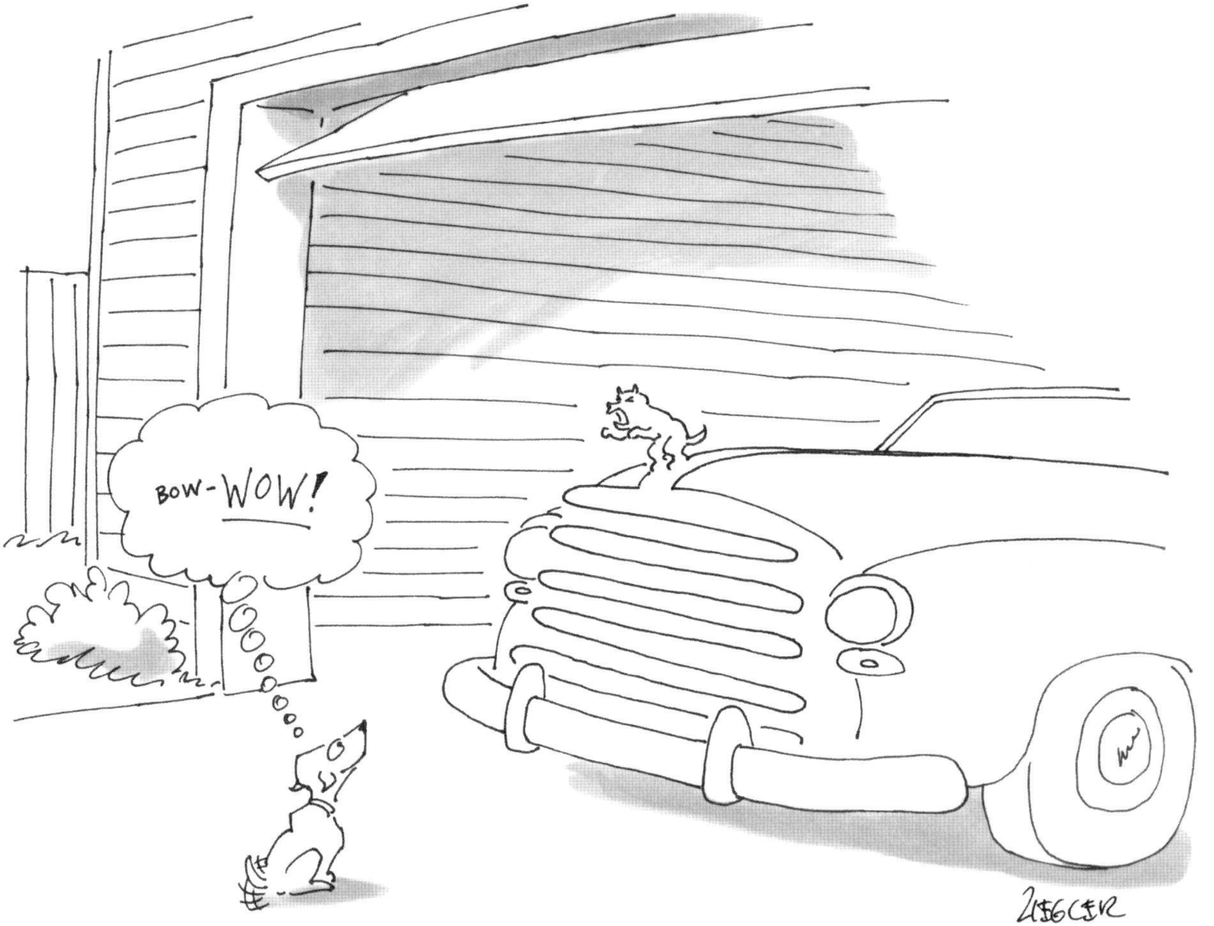
BOW-WOW!

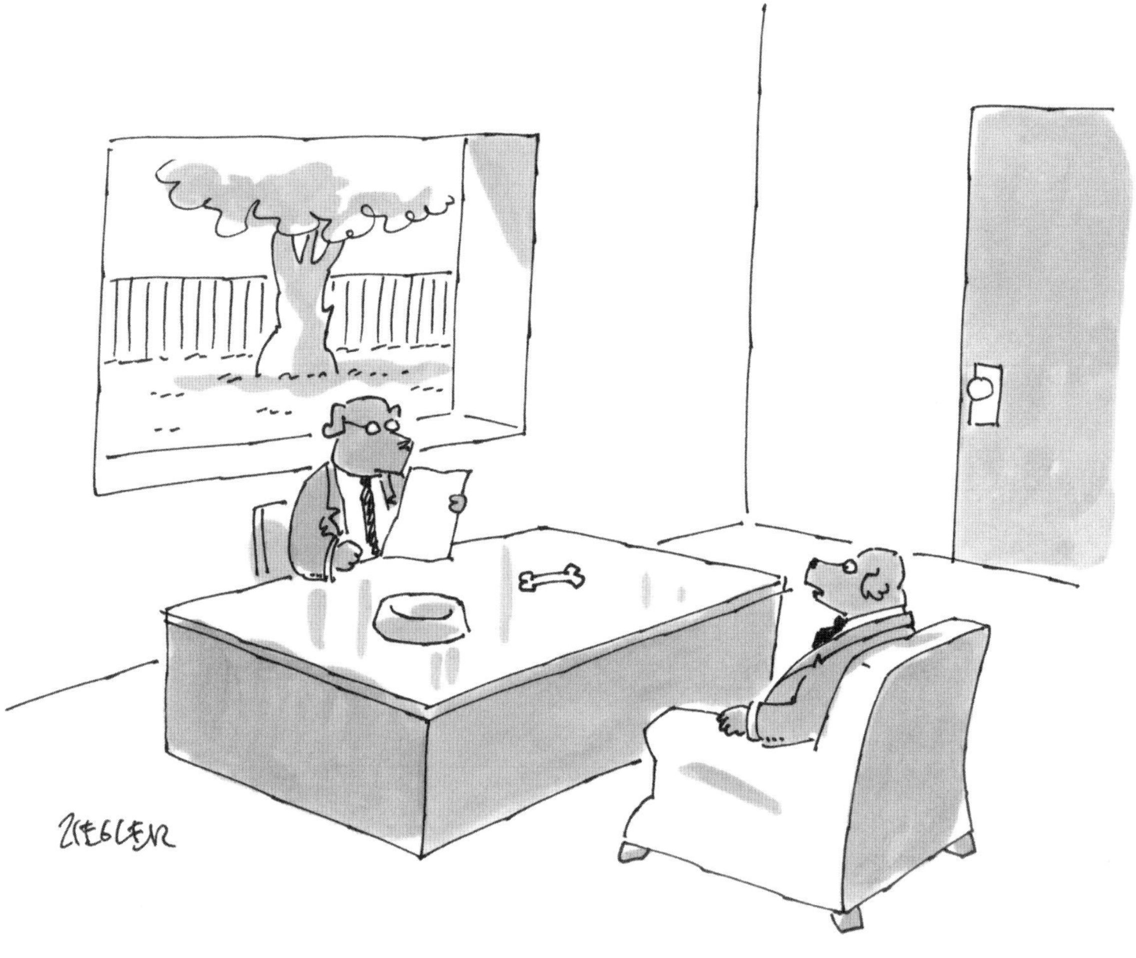
ZIEGLER

"You'll notice on my resumé that I'm pretty good at chasing sticks, and I think that ability may pay off someday in a not insubstantial way."

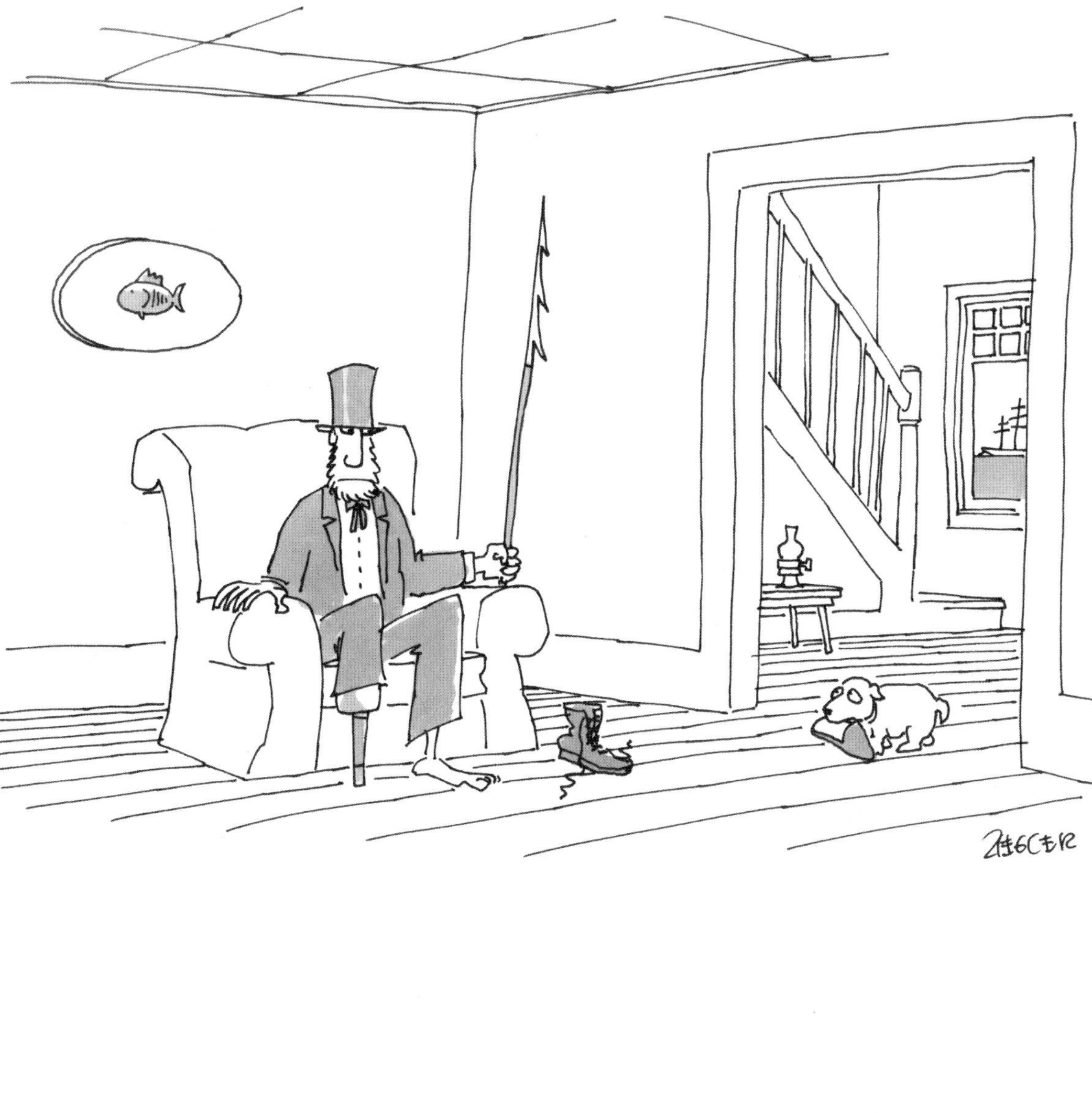
ZIEGLER

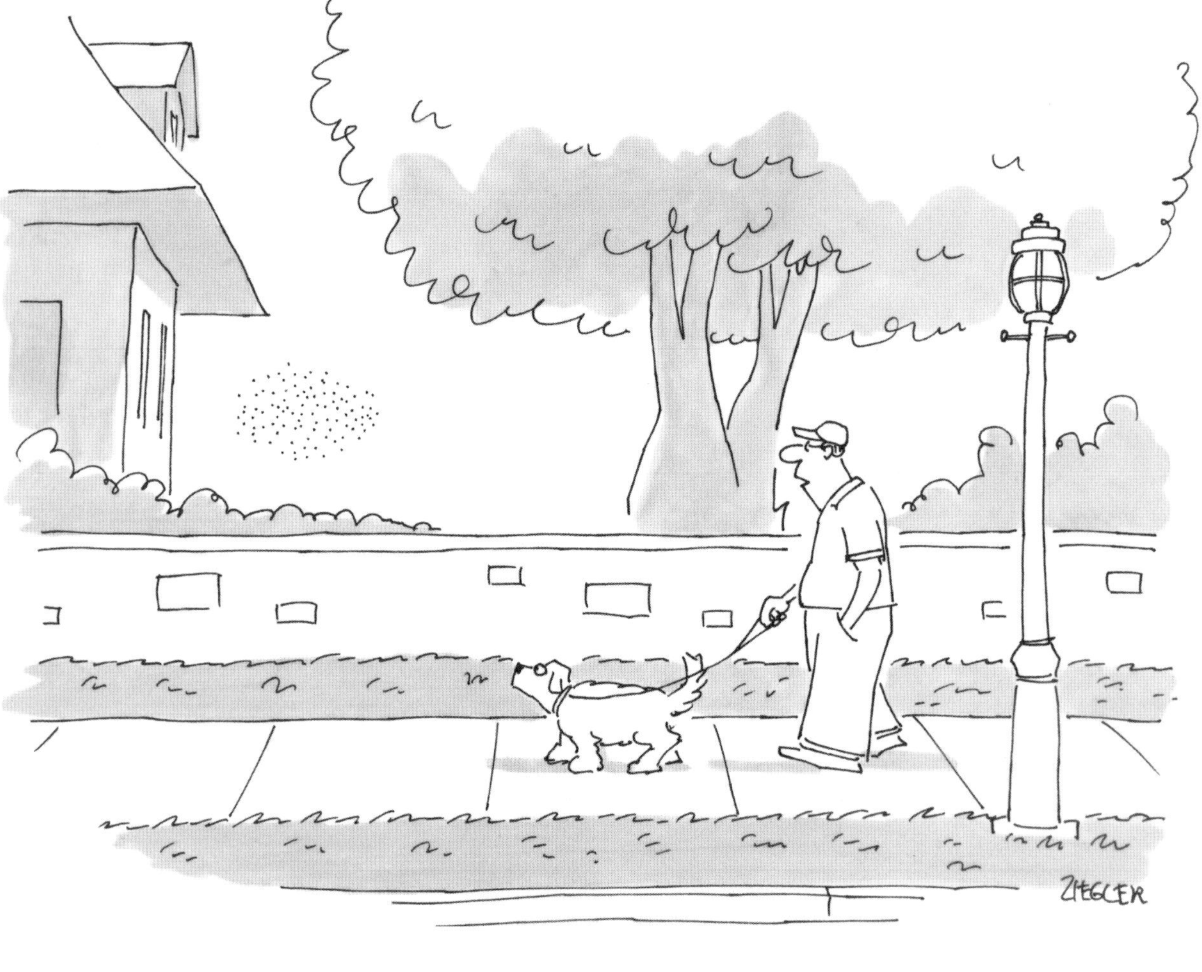
ZIEGLER

"Cluster of gnats at two o'clock. Prepare for evasive action."

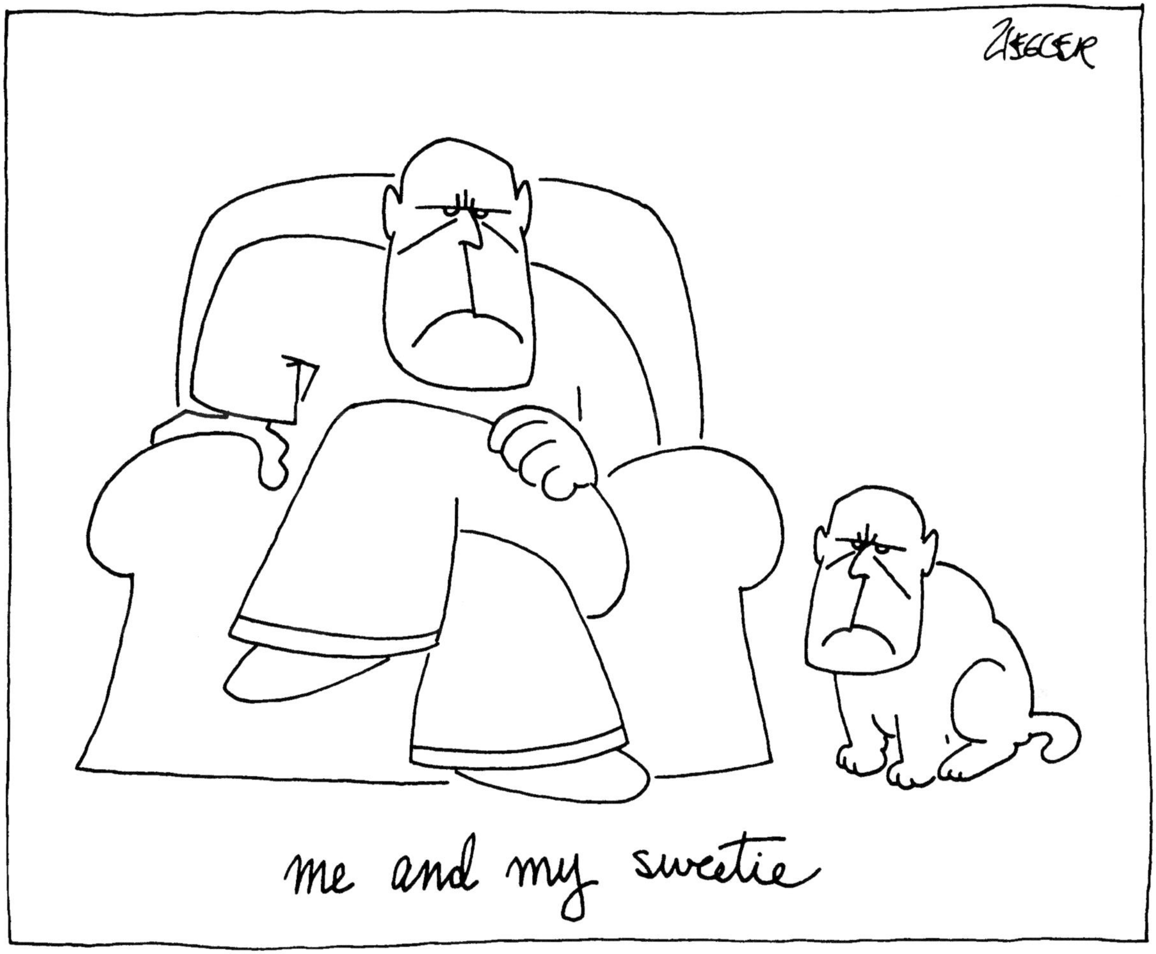
ZIEGLER
me and my sweetie

"__Good__ doggie!"

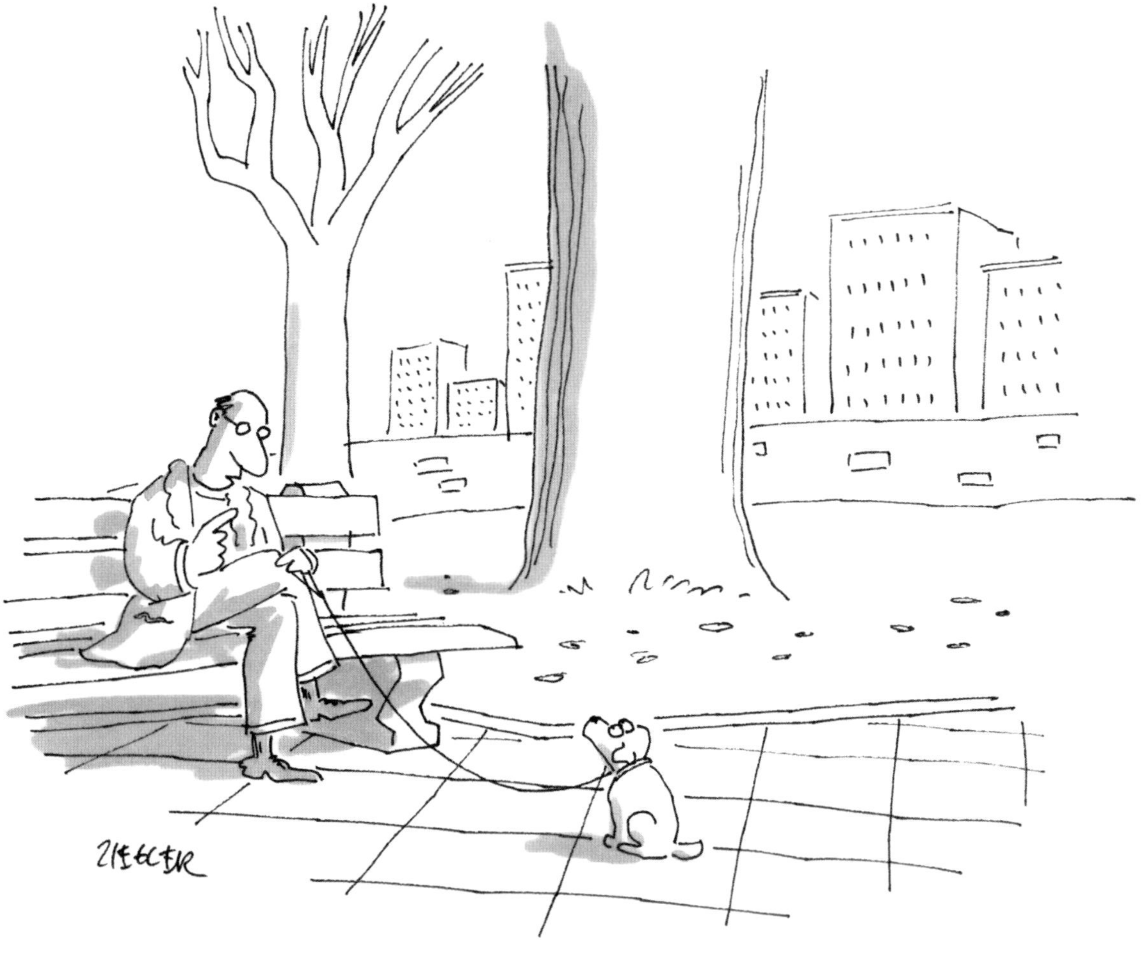
ZIEGLER

"In another billion years or so, Taffy, when you have evolved further, you, too, may sit on the bench."

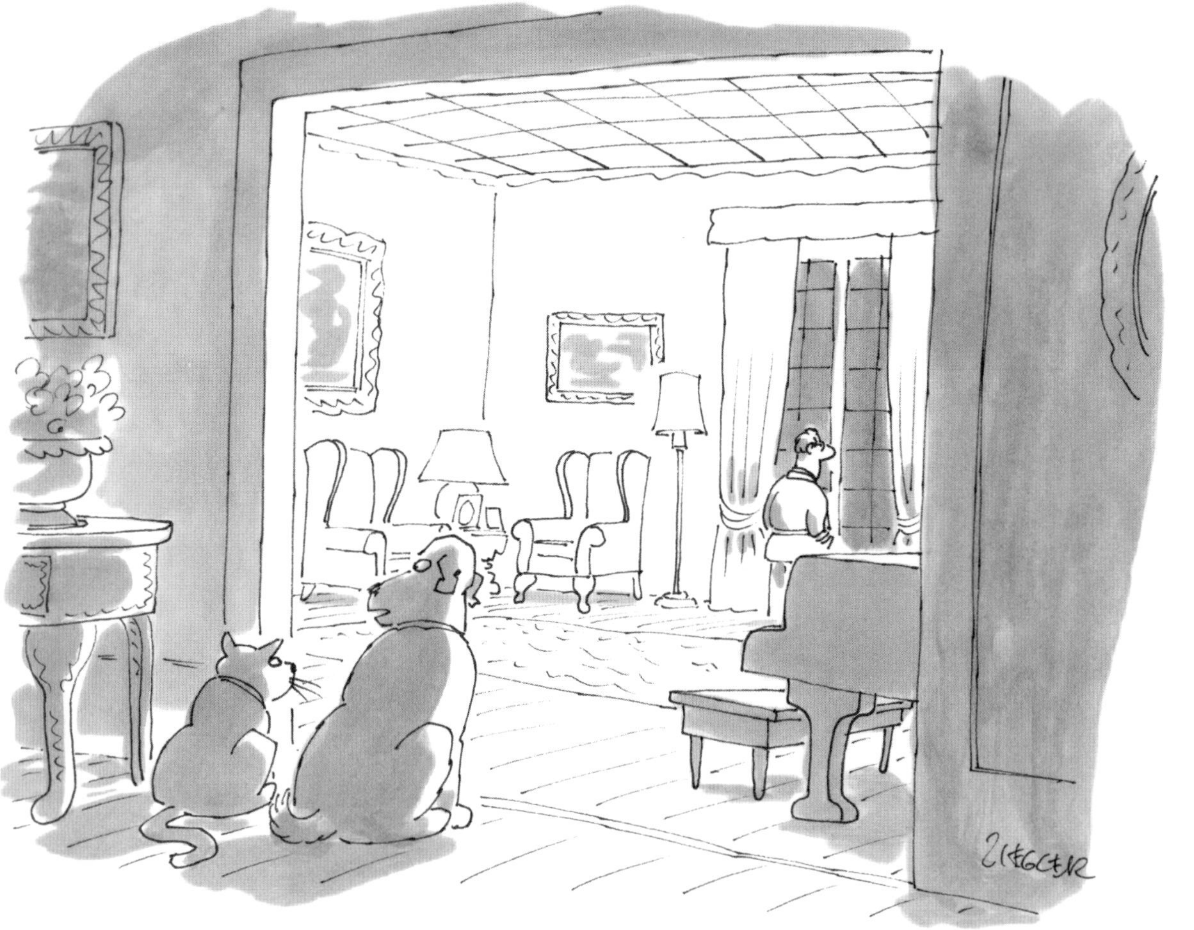
ZIEGLER

"Our master's lowly bipedal status greatly impedes his ability to succeed."

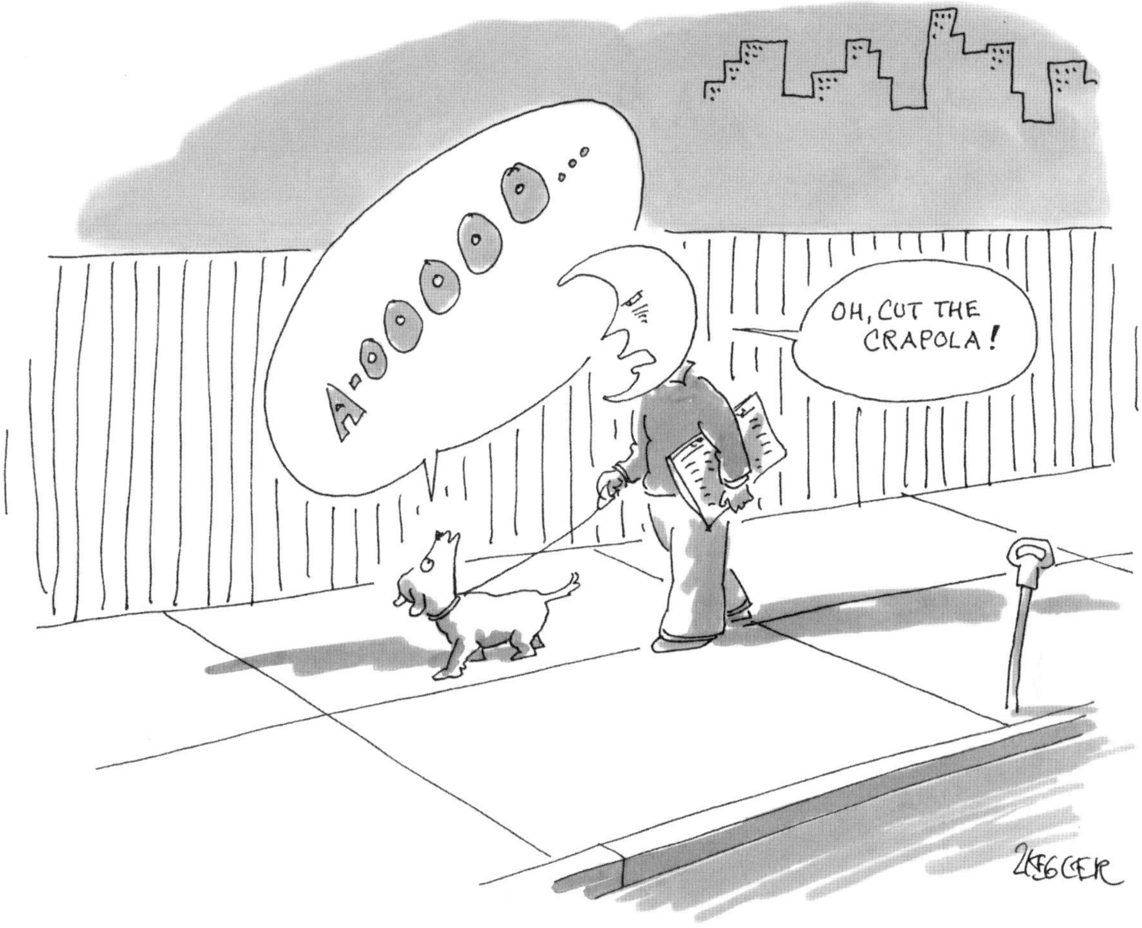
A-OOOOO...
OH, CUT THE CRAPOLA!
ZIEGLER

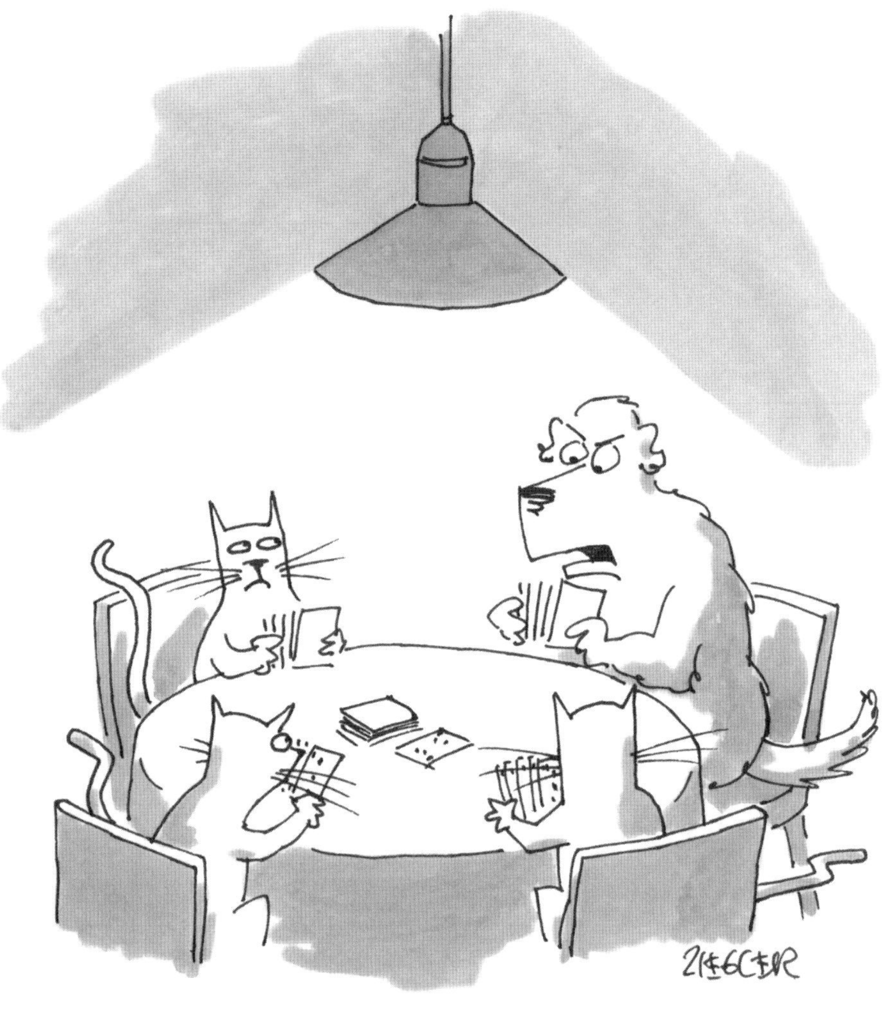
ZIEGLER

"Who dealt this mess?"

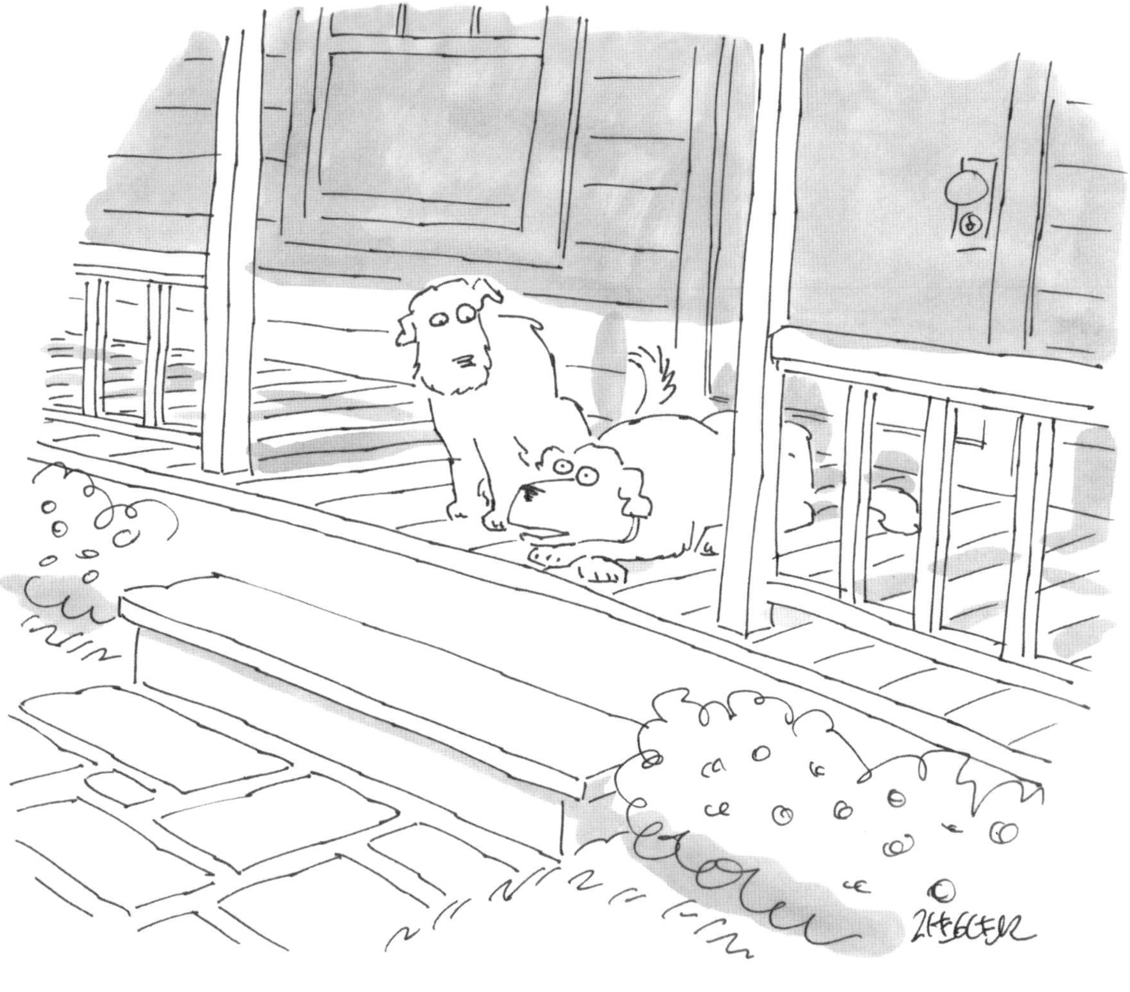
ZIEGLER

"When my master died, I mourned—and I continued to mourn even as I dined on his savory and scrumptious thigh."

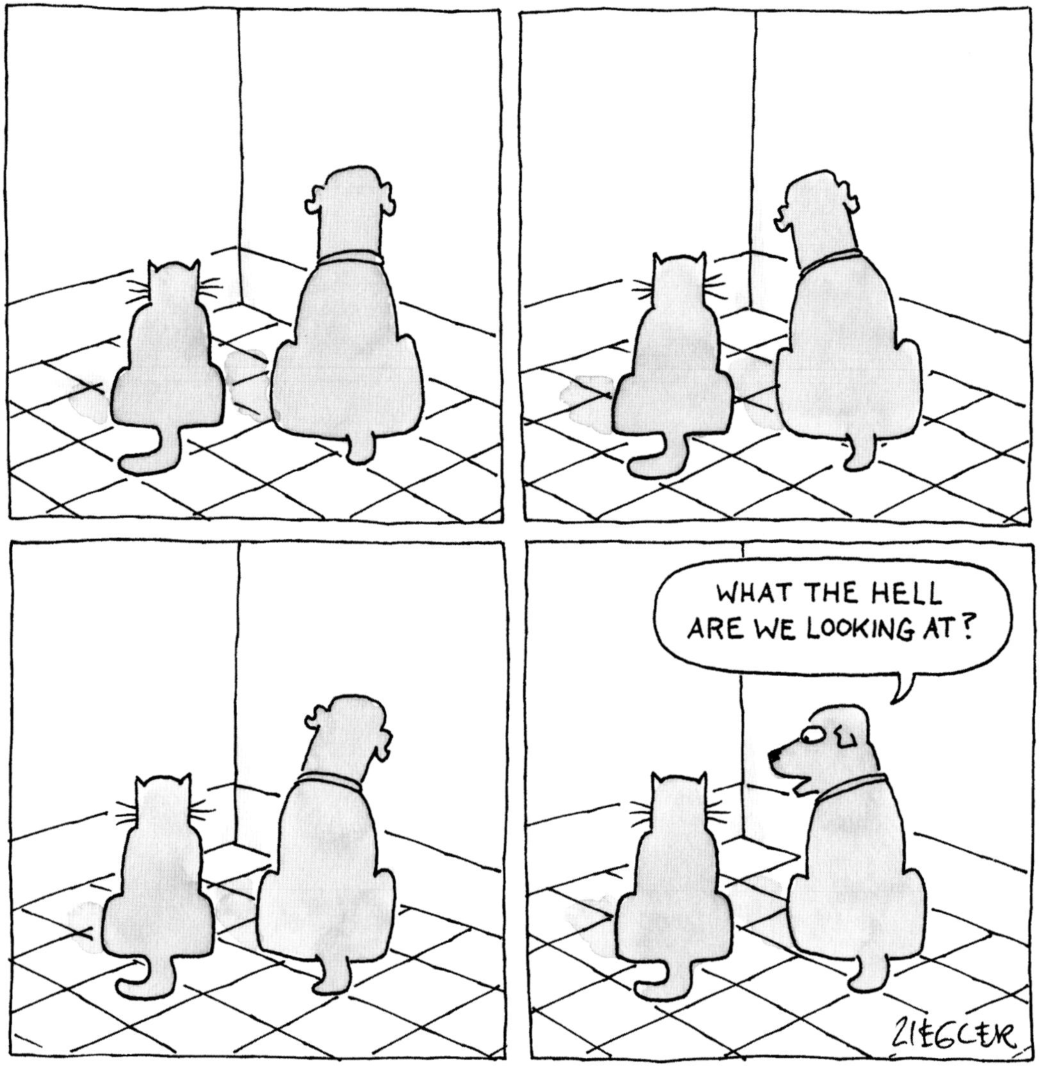
WHAT THE HELL
ARE WE LOOKING AT?
ZIEGLER

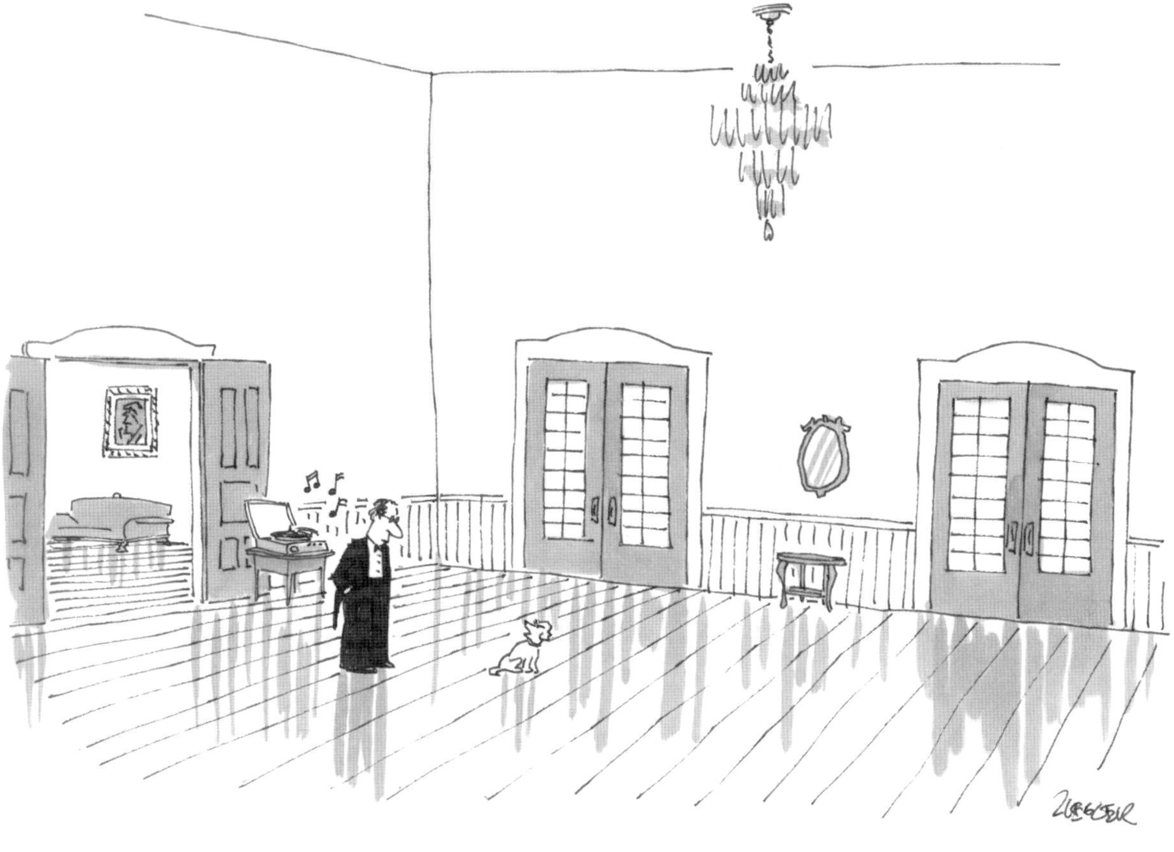
ZIEGLER

"I don't do the fox trot. I don't do the monkey. And I don't do the fish. I do the dog."

"She's been spayed and I've been fixed, so I'm pretty sure we're going to go platonic."

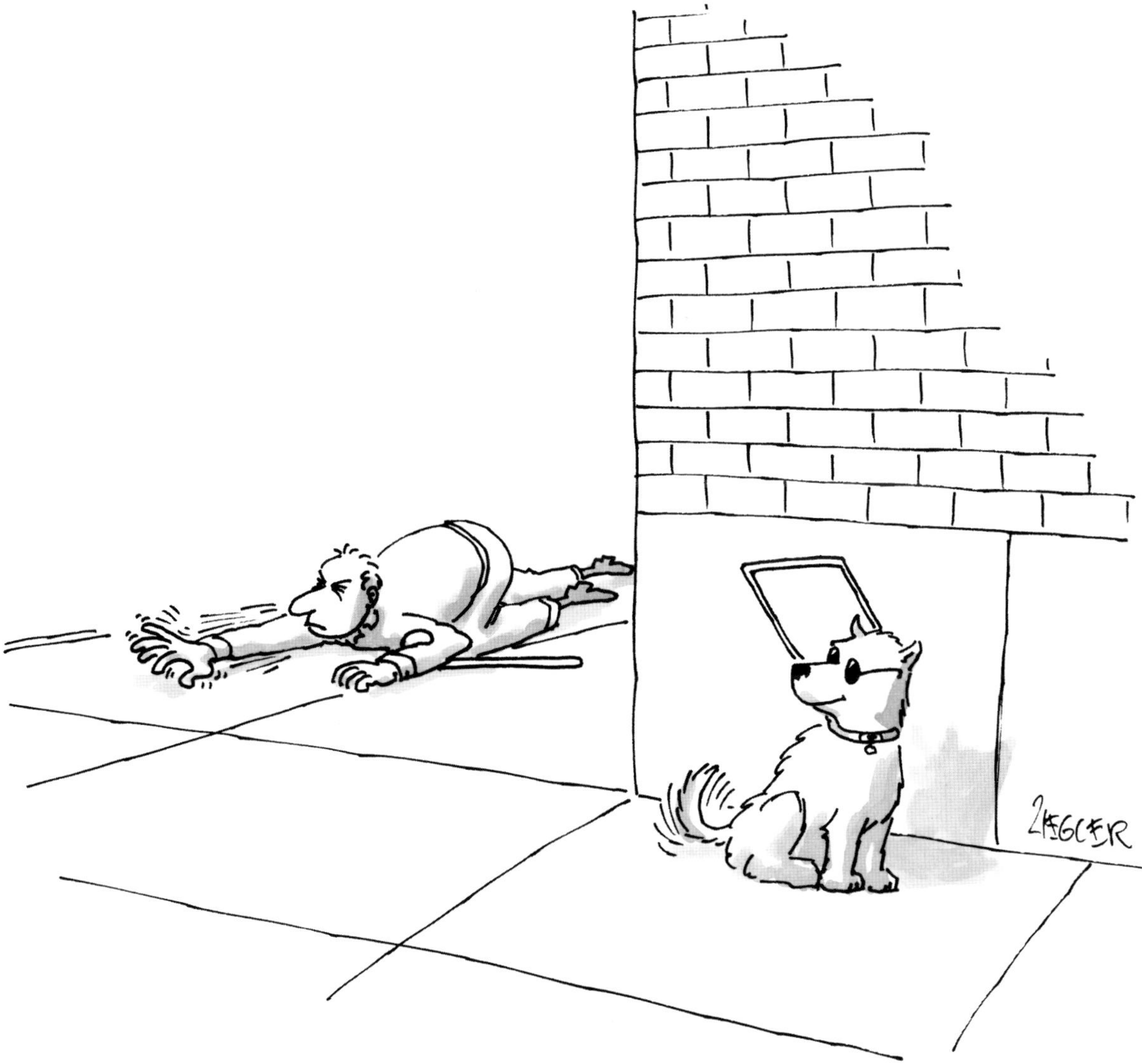

"For the billionth damn time, we have to wait to be buzzed in!"

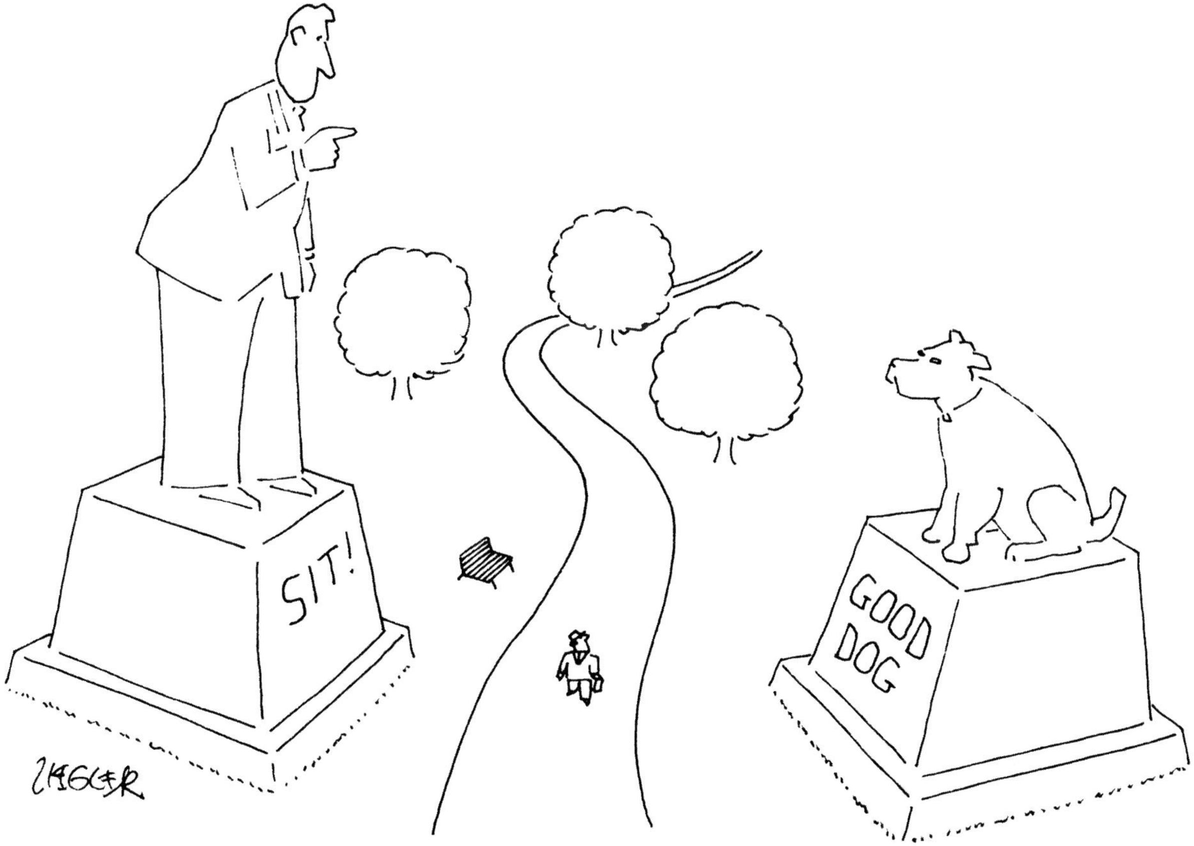
SIT!
GOOD DOG
ZIEGLER

"I came across a hair in my food today, but it was O.K., as it did not appear to be human."

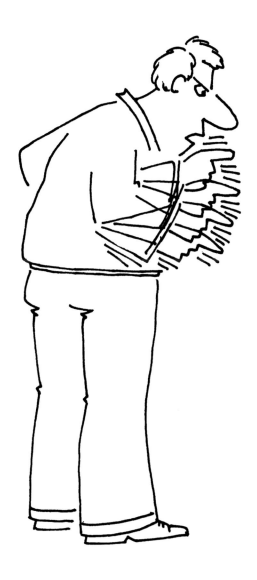

"You have the kind of look that I really go for, dollface.
Do you also by any chance happen to have papers?"

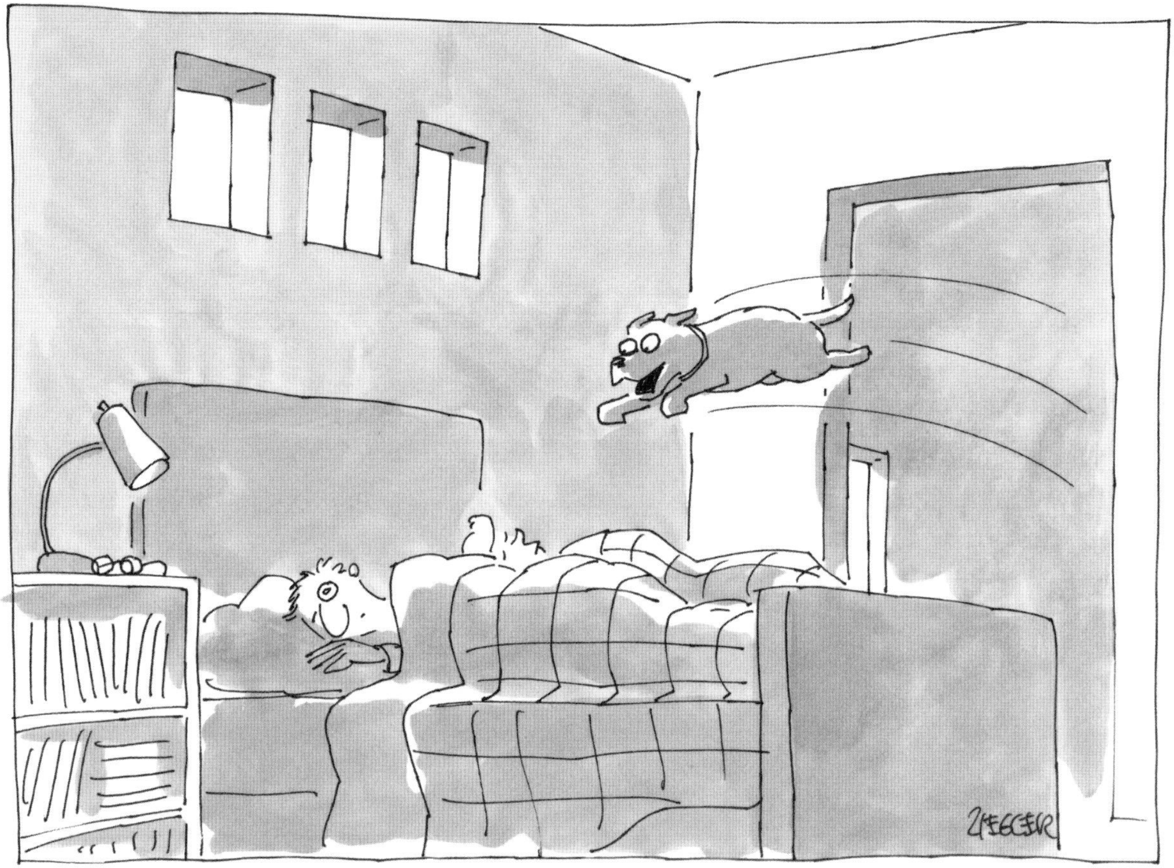
ZIEGLER

THE SIXTY–FIVE–POUND ALARM CLOCK

"*They're back! They're back! How do I look? Oh, never mind! <u>Never mind!</u>*"

"It's been my experience that using all four appendages is helpful."

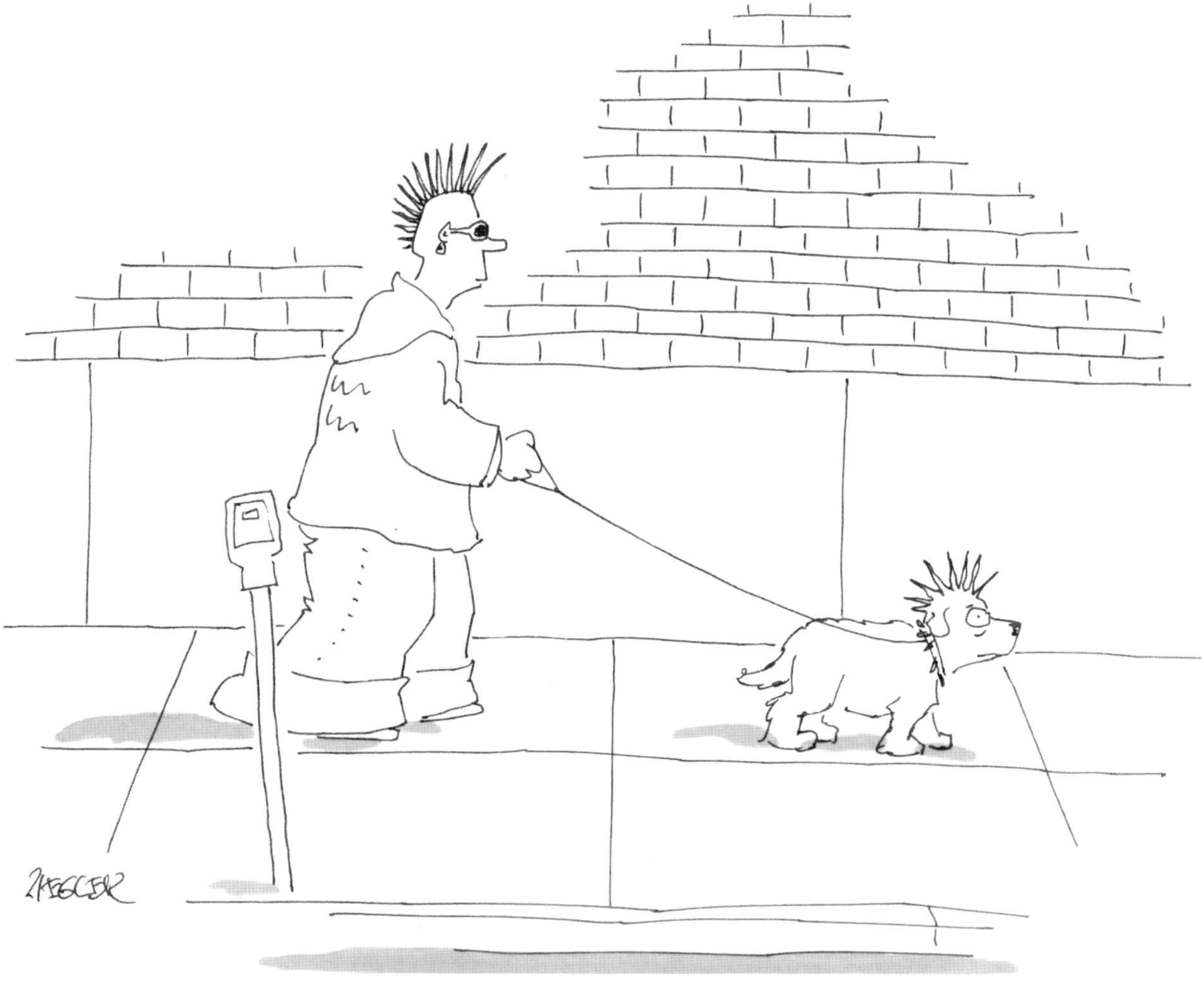

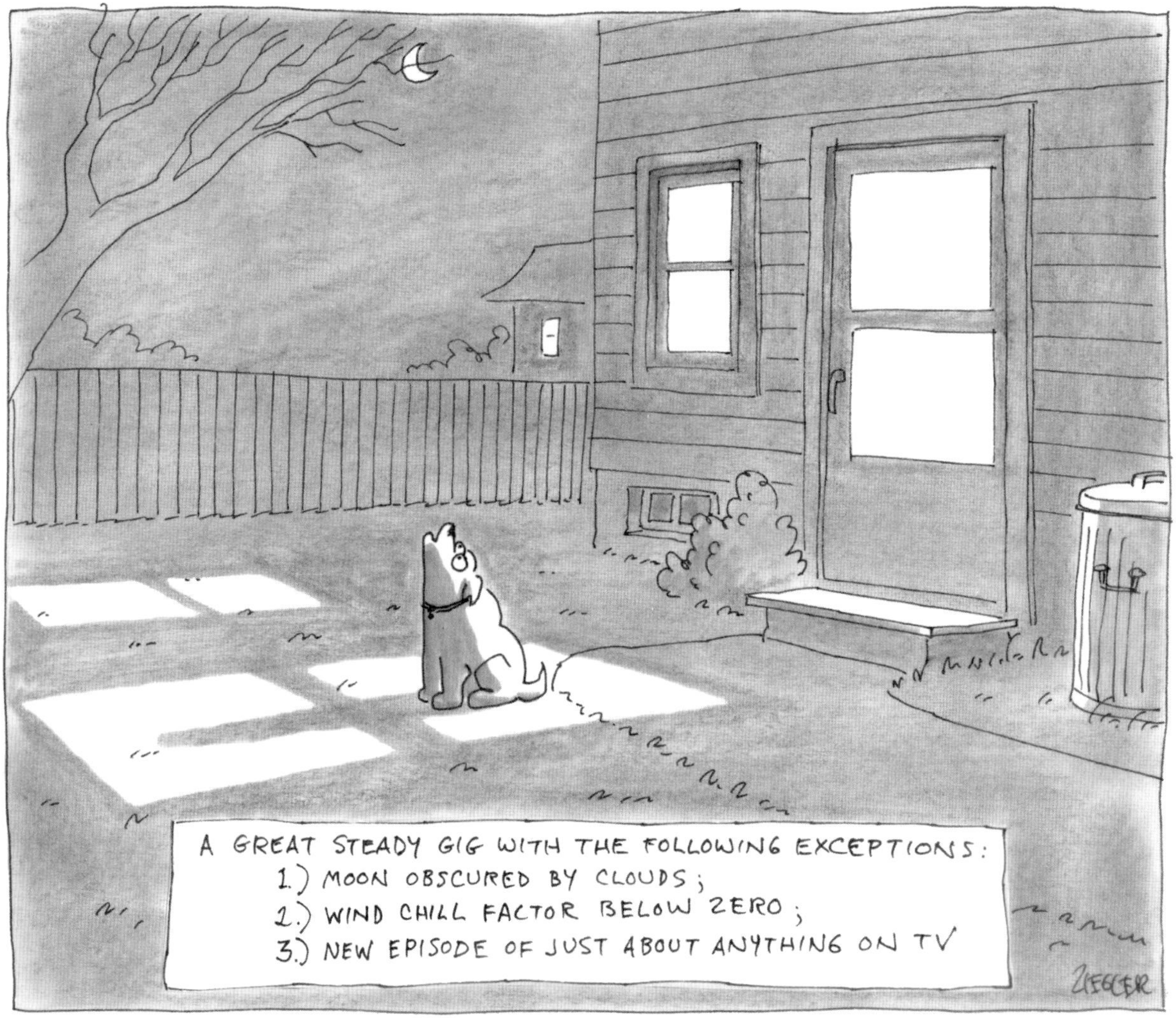
A GREAT STEADY GIG WITH THE FOLLOWING EXCEPTIONS:
1.) MOON OBSCURED BY CLOUDS;
2.) WIND CHILL FACTOR BELOW ZERO;
3.) NEW EPISODE OF JUST ABOUT ANYTHING ON TV
ZIEGLER

"I hate them all, but their catnip is to die for."

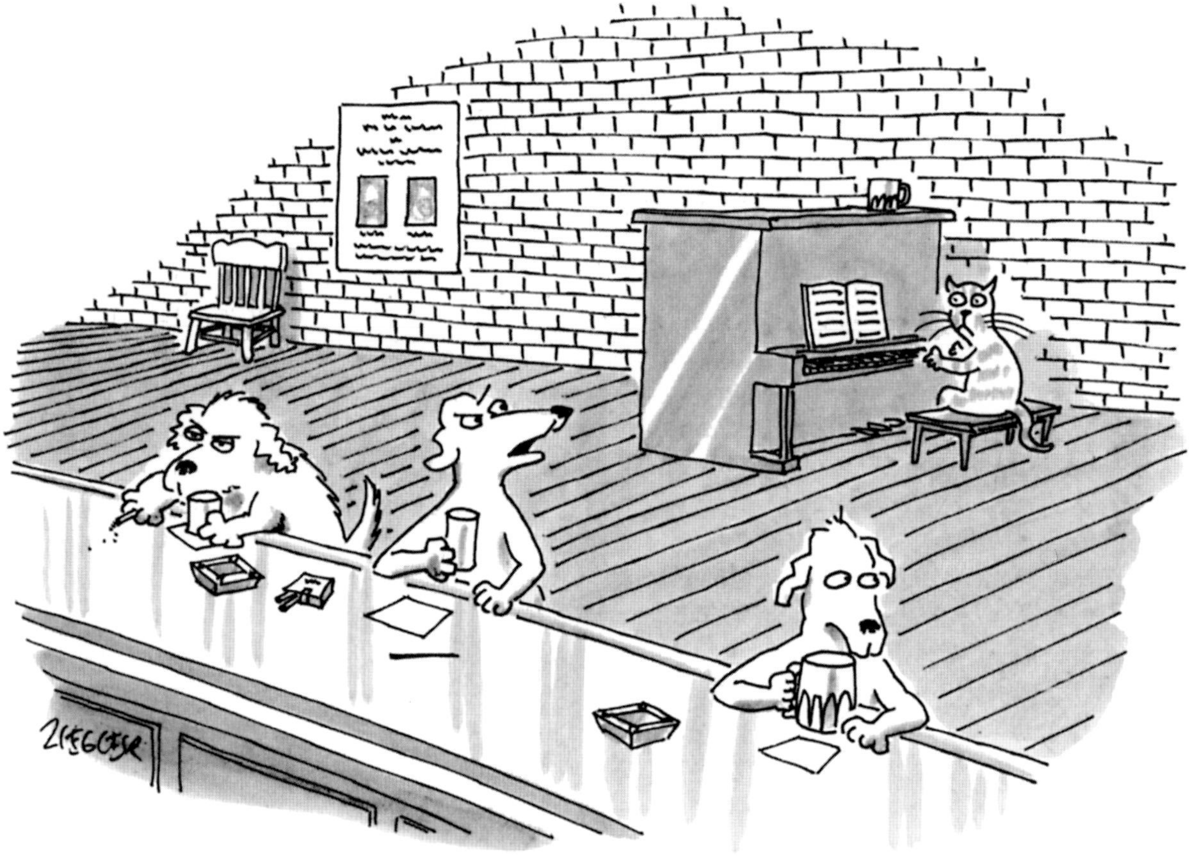
ZIEGLER

"Hey, pal, let's hear 'Doggie in the Window' again, and this time play it like you mean it!"

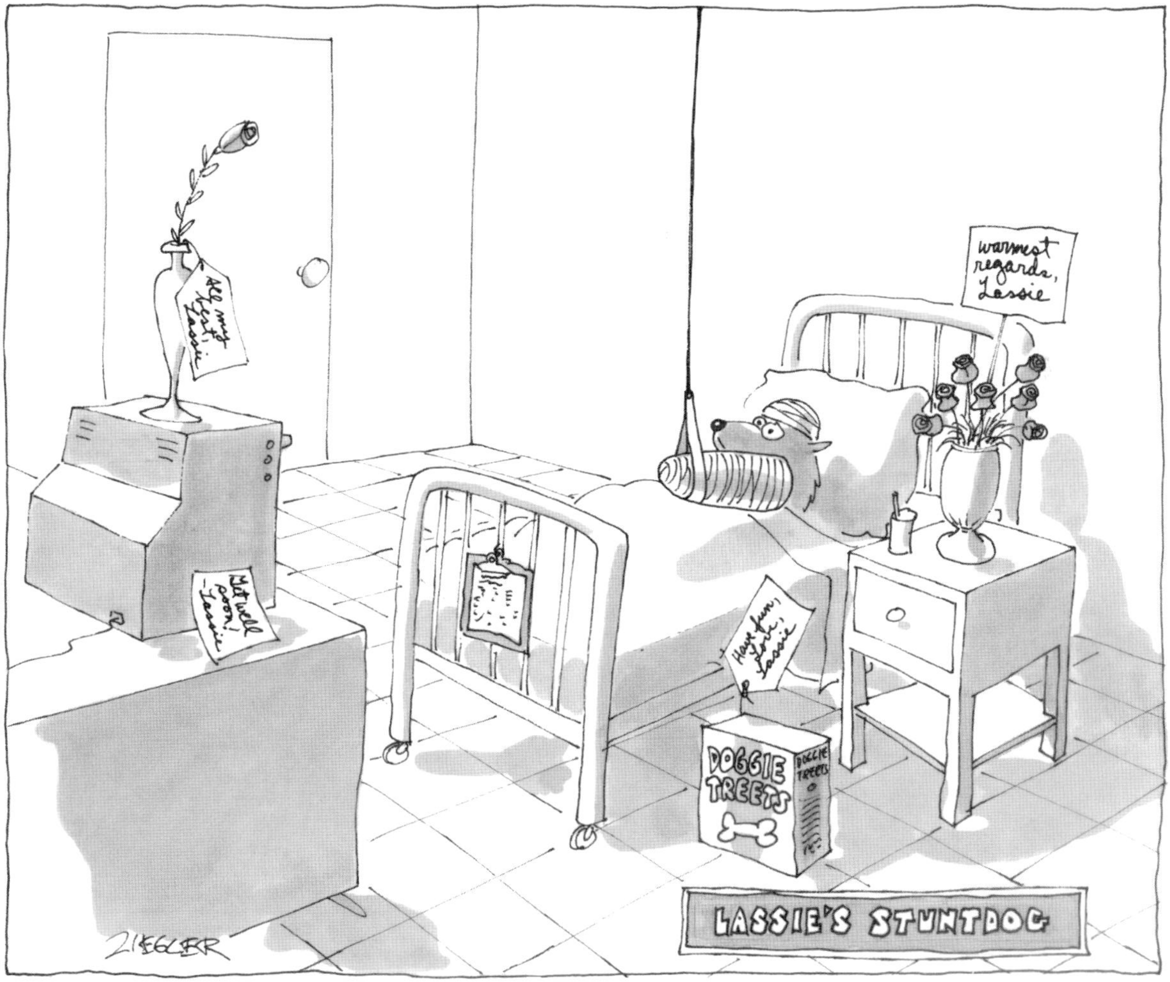
All my best, Lassie
warmest regards, Lassie
Get well soon! —Lassie
Have fun, Love, Lassie
DOGGIE TREETS
LASSIE'S STUNTDOG
ZIEGLER

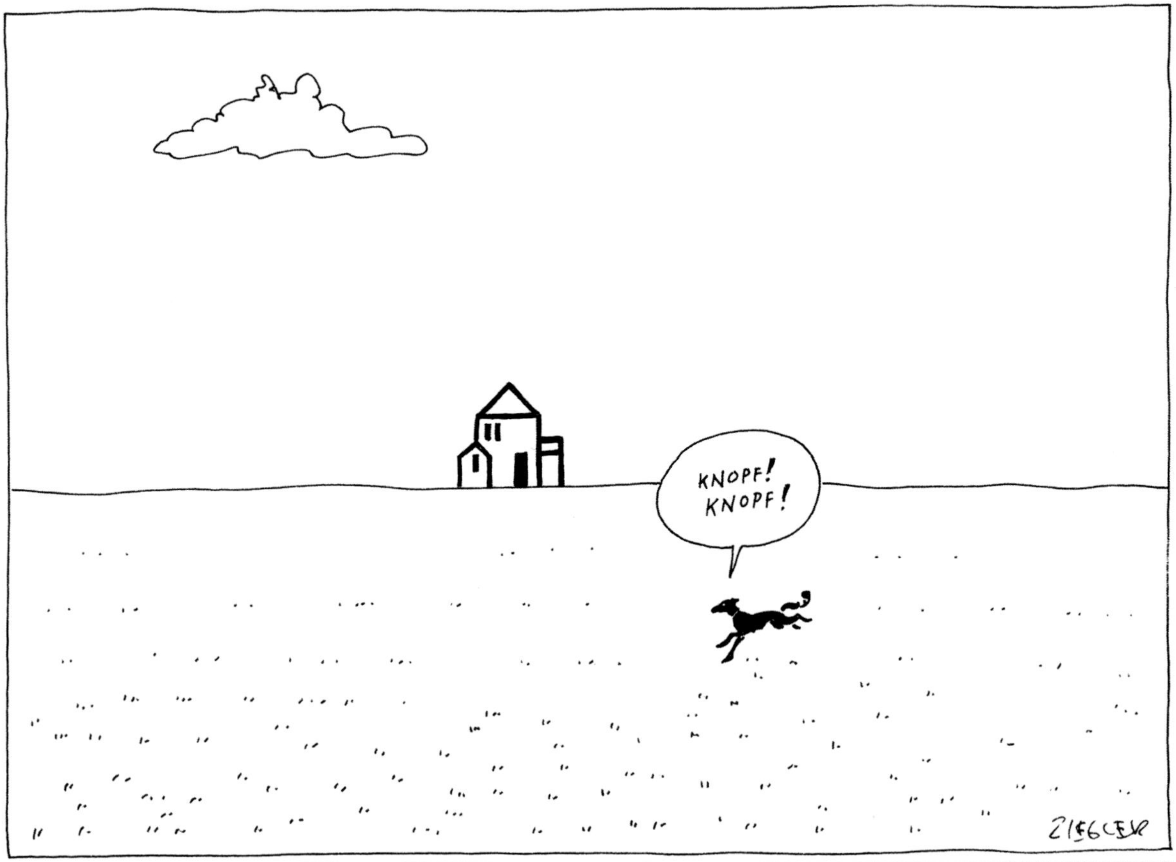
KNOPF! KNOPF!
ZIEGLER

THE RANDOM HOUSE ON THE PRAIRIE UNDER DURESS FROM SOME NEIGHBOR'S INTRUSIVE DOG

"Hard to believe, isn't it?, that in China they gobble these things up like candy."

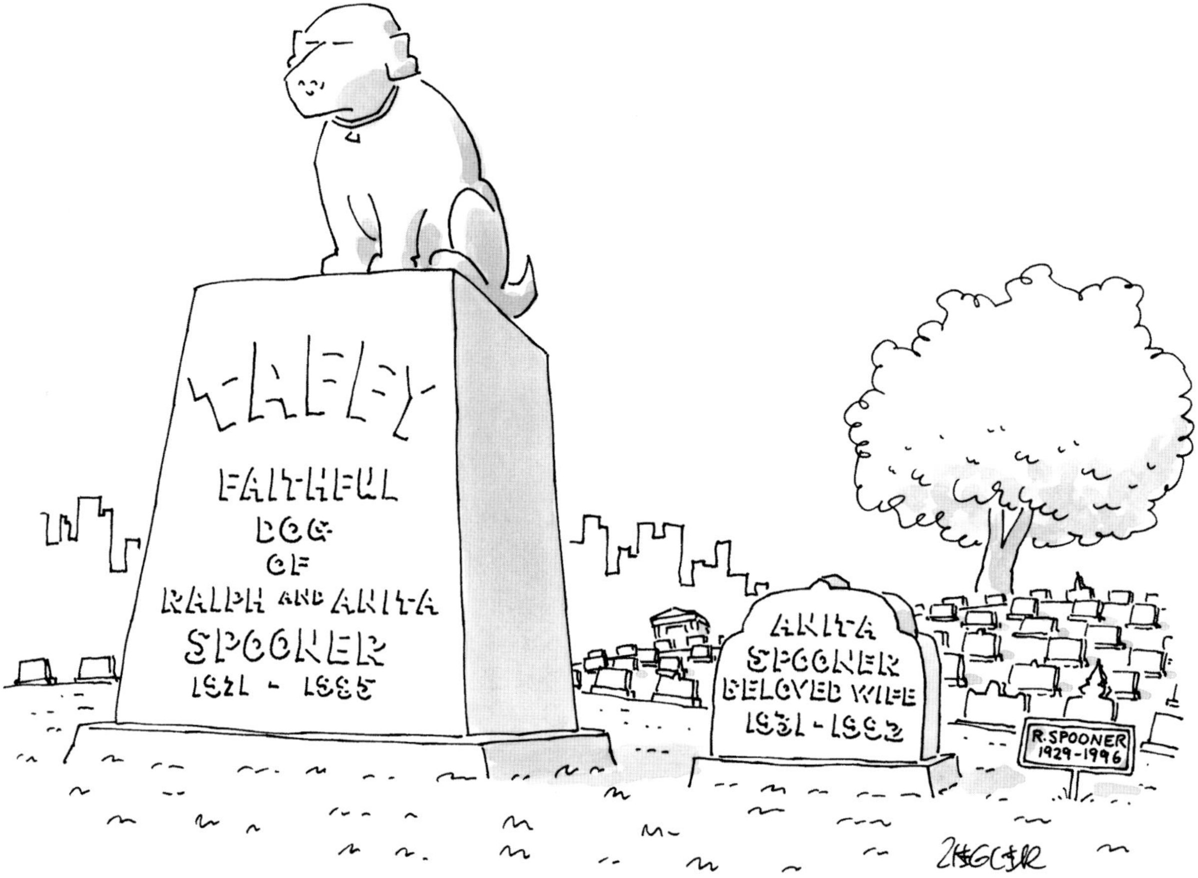
TAFFY
FAITHFUL
DOG
OF
RALPH AND ANITA
SPOONER
ANITA
SPOONER
BELOVED WIFE
R. SPOONER
1929-1996

"They say that every dog has its day, and this apparently is mine."

"Where's Fluffy? Go play with your friend Fluffy."

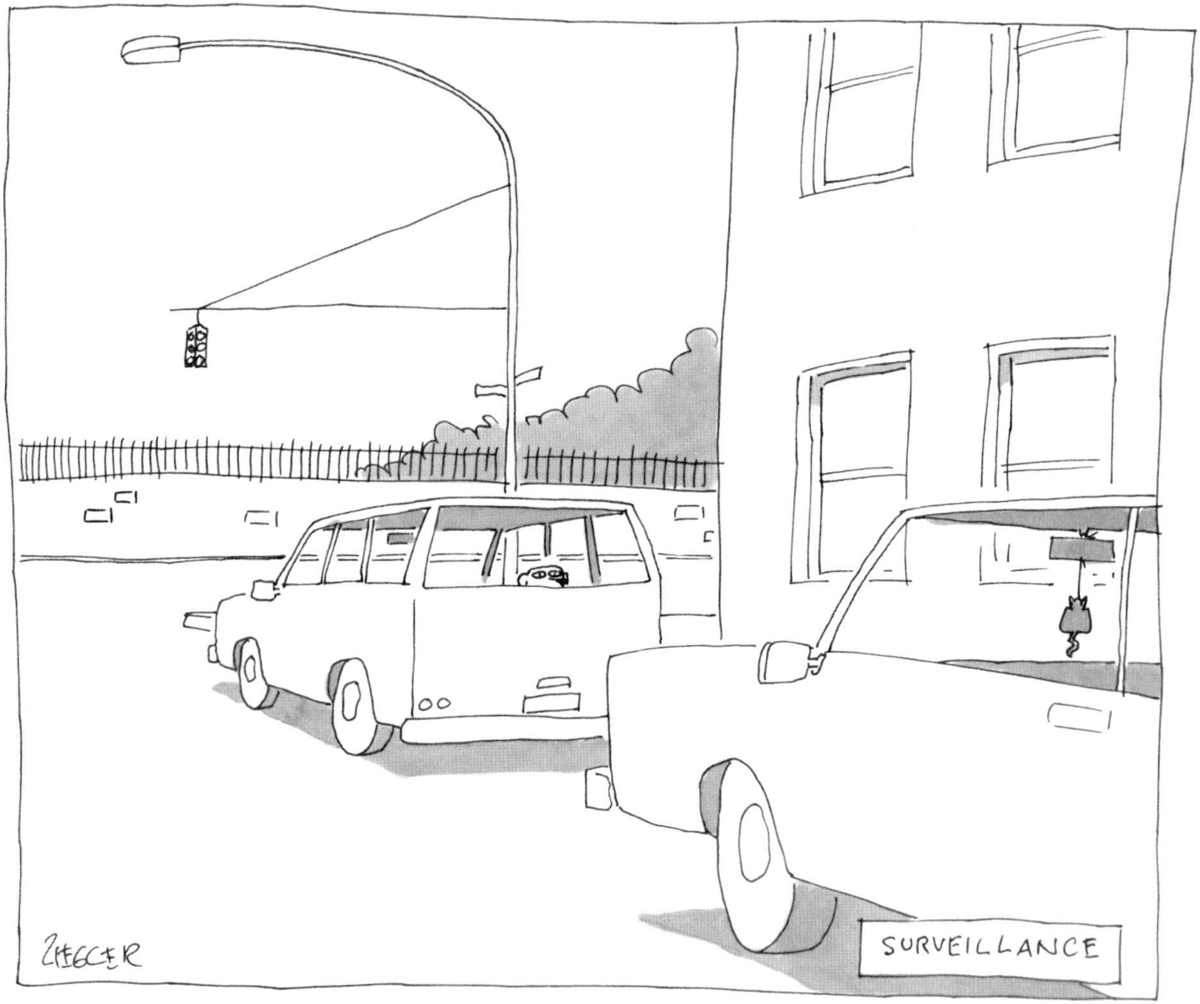
SURVEILLANCE

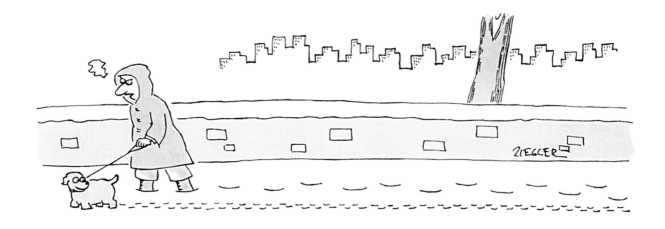

"Can we forget about our dainty little tracks in the snow for five seconds and try to concentrate on what we're out here for?"

"How come *you* never come up with any *stupid pet tricks?*"

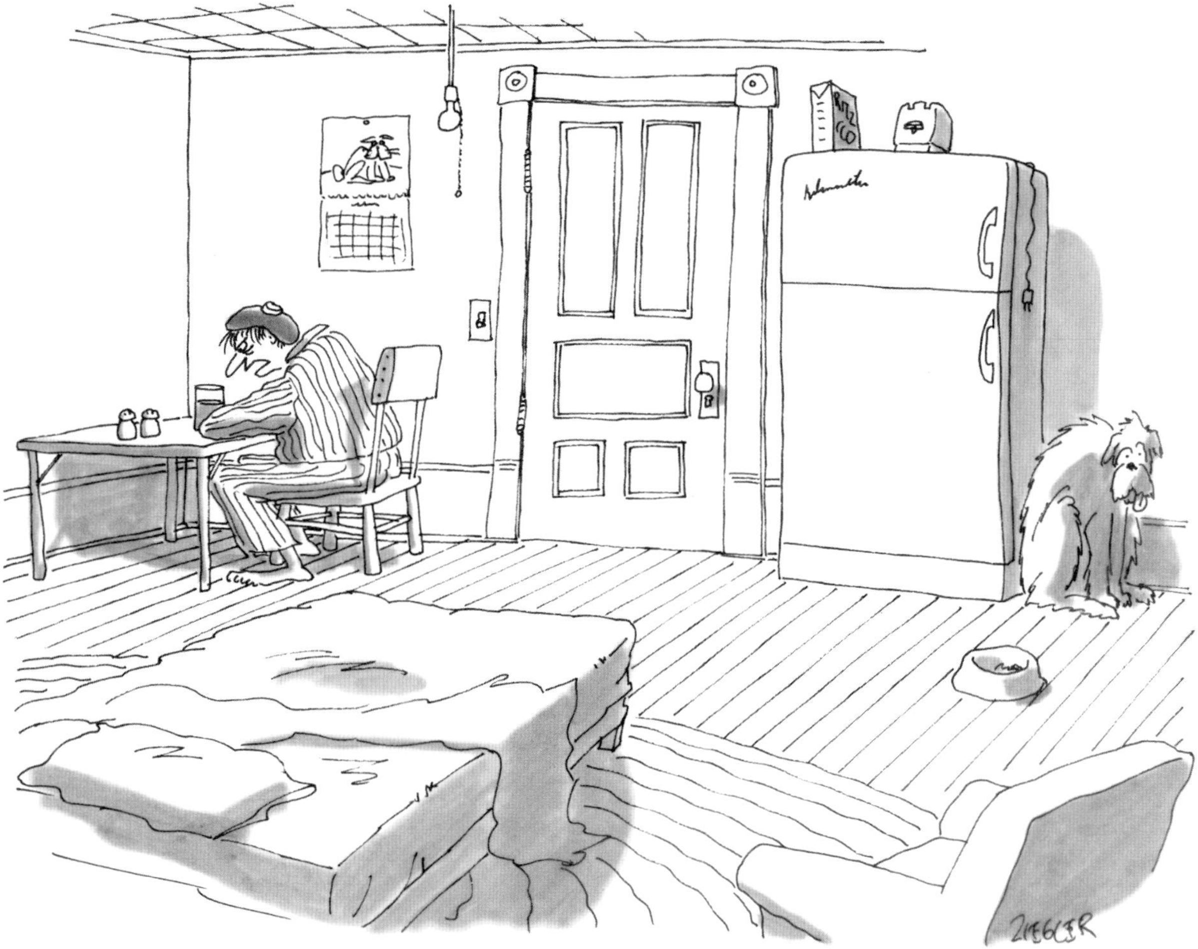
ZIEGLER

"Tippy! I hope these aren't dog hairs in my hair of the dog again!"

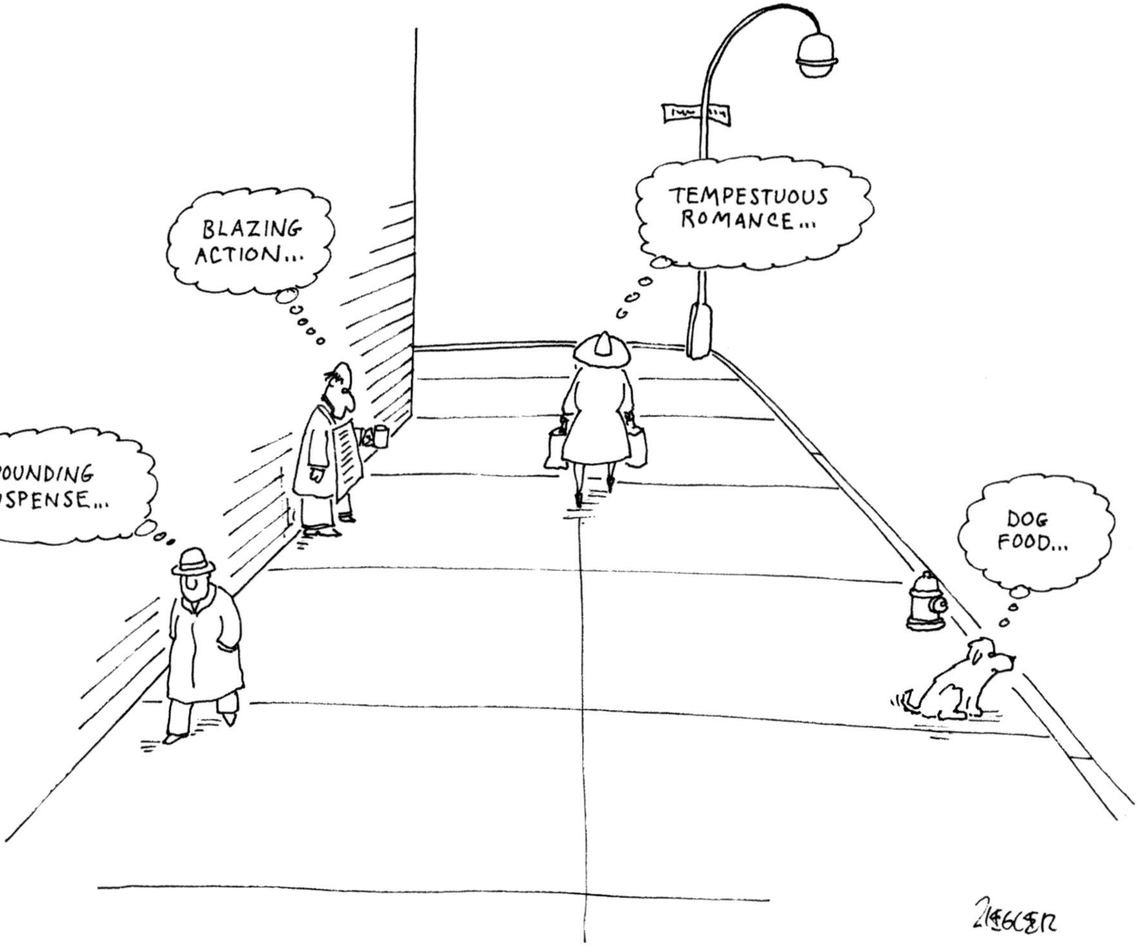
BLAZING ACTION...
TEMPESTUOUS ROMANCE...
POUNDING SUSPENSE...
DOG FOOD...
ZIEGLER

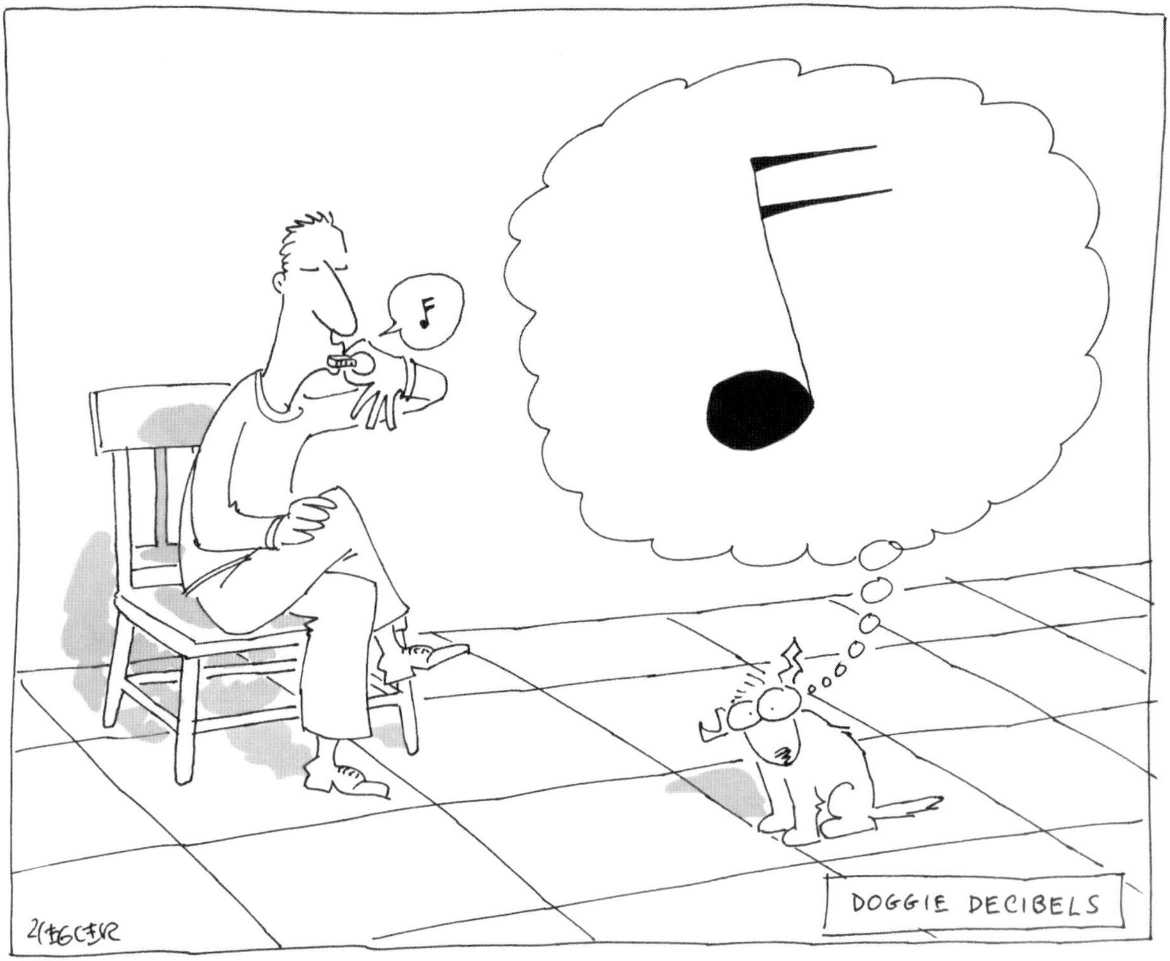
DOGGIE DECIBELS
ZIEGLER

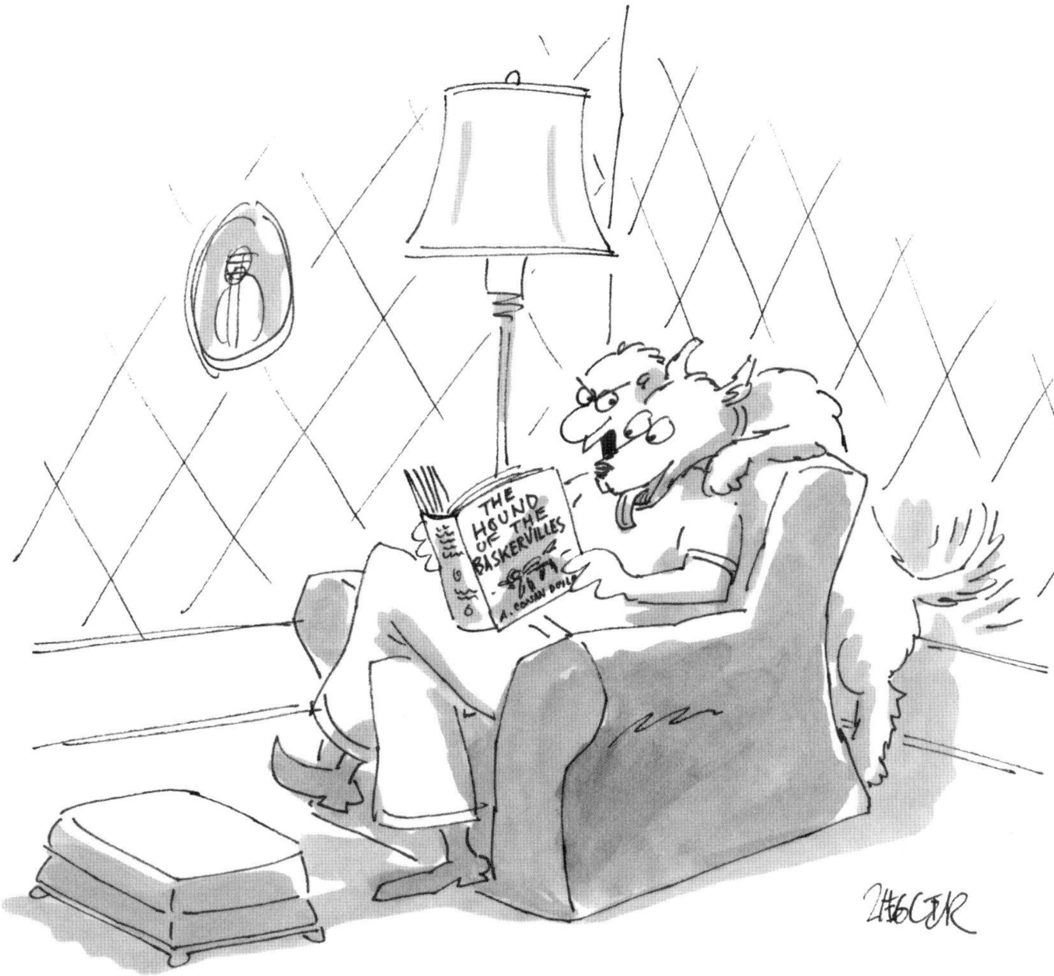
THE HOUND OF THE BASKERVILLES
A. CONAN DOYLE

"Is it O.K. with you if I turn the page yet?"

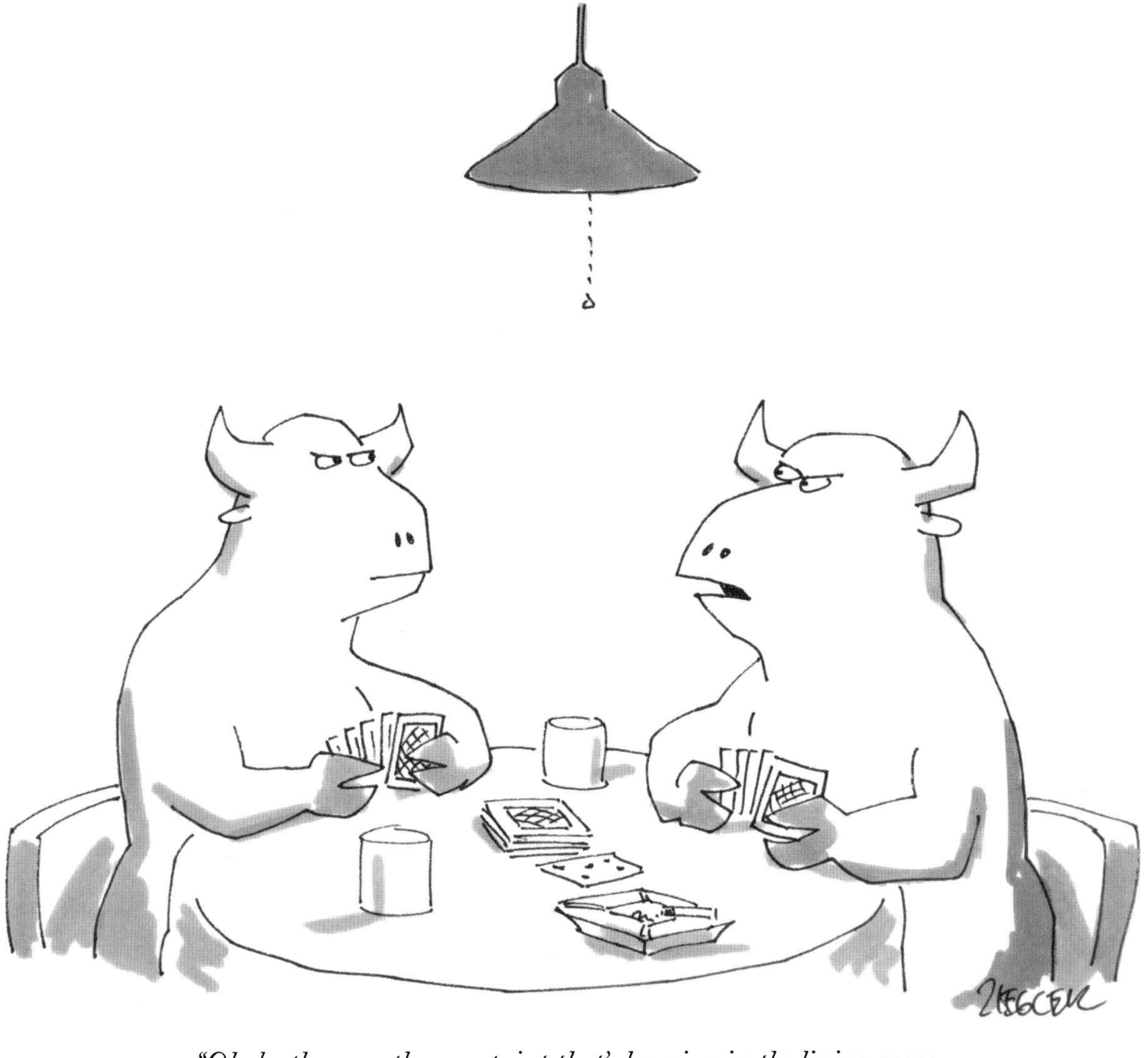
ZIEGLER

"Oh, by the way, the new print that's hanging in the living room. The one with the dogs playing cards. It's stupid."

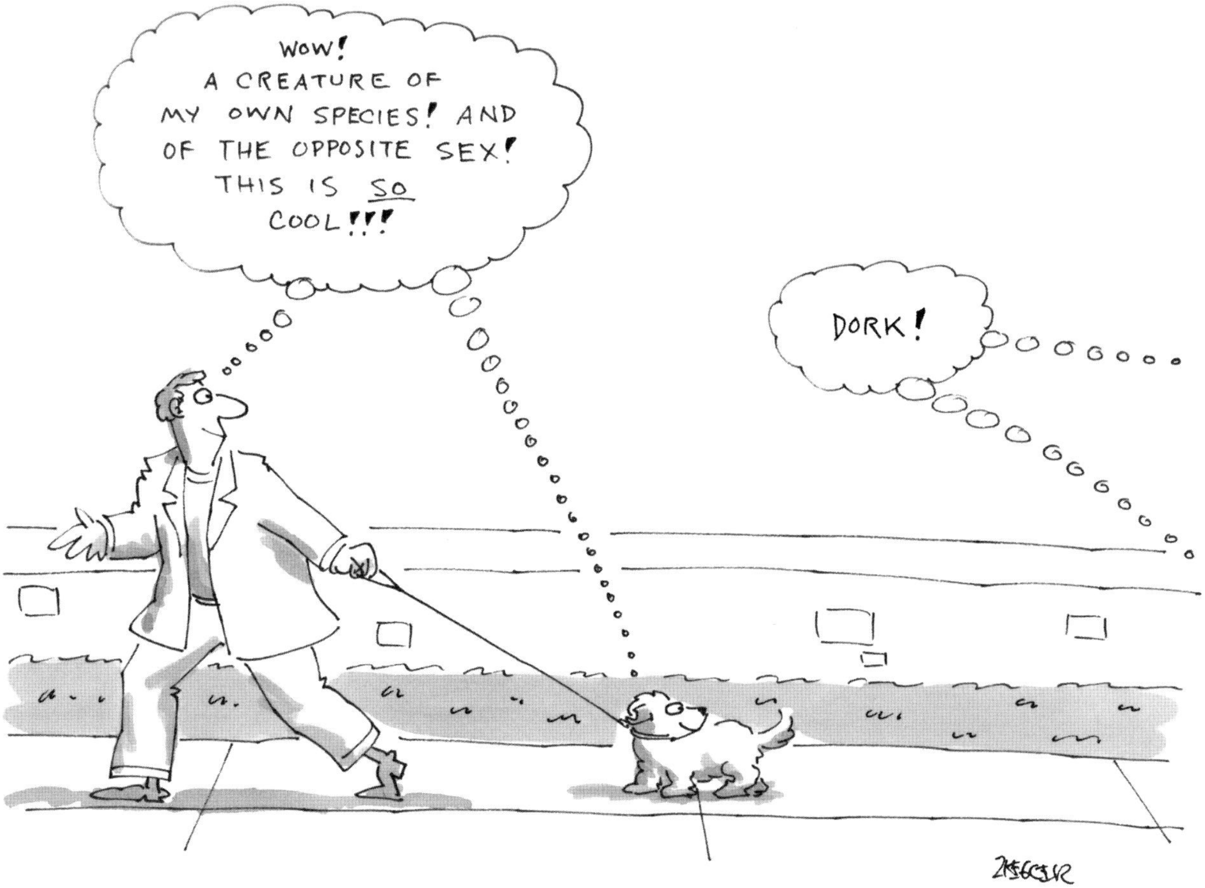
WOW!
A CREATURE OF
MY OWN SPECIES! AND
OF THE OPPOSITE SEX!
THIS IS SO
COOL!!!
DORK!

"Excuse me, but I wasn't speaking to you. I was speaking to that fellow up there."

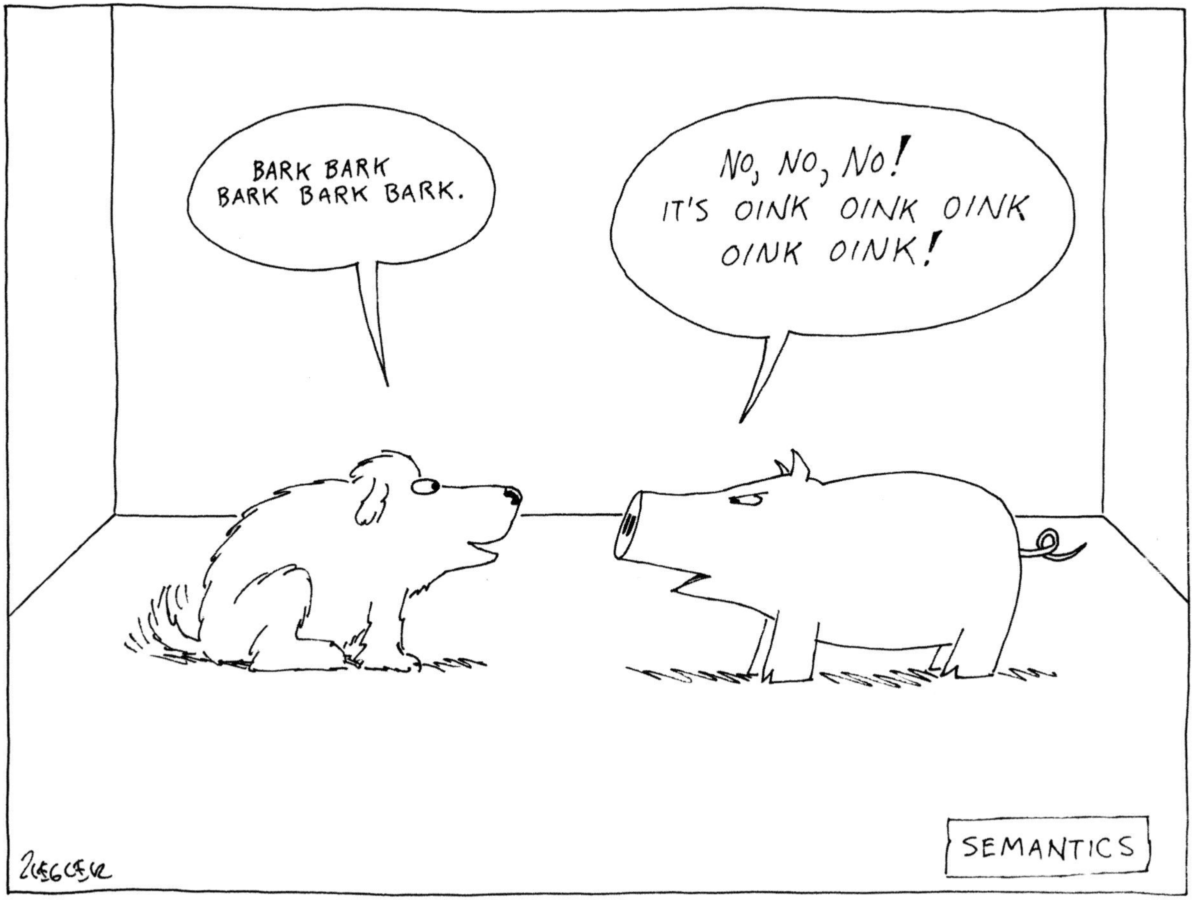
BARK BARK
BARK BARK BARK.
No, No, No!
IT'S OINK OINK OINK
OINK OINK!
SEMANTICS

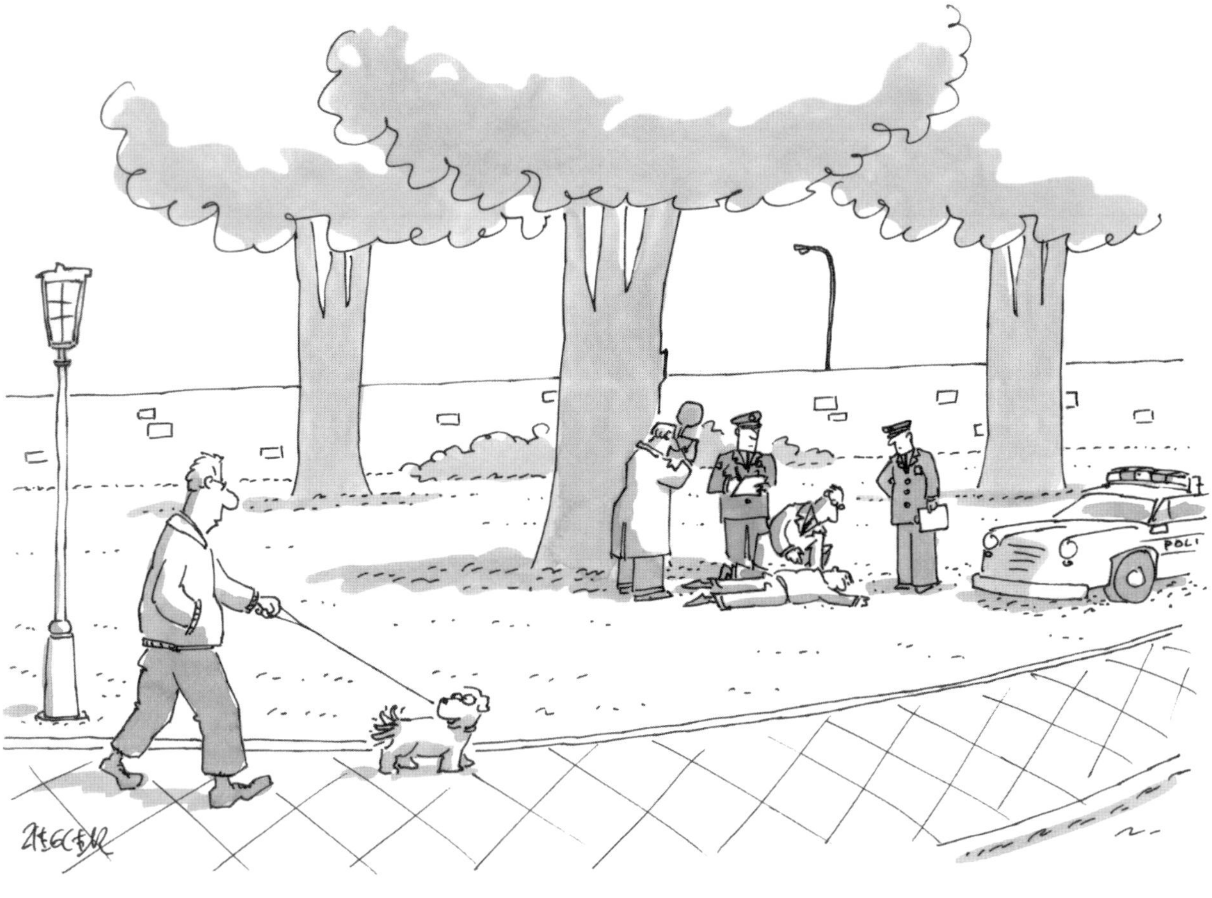
POLI

"No, Sparky. Those people don't have time to play right now."

"Come on! It's supposed to be good for you!"

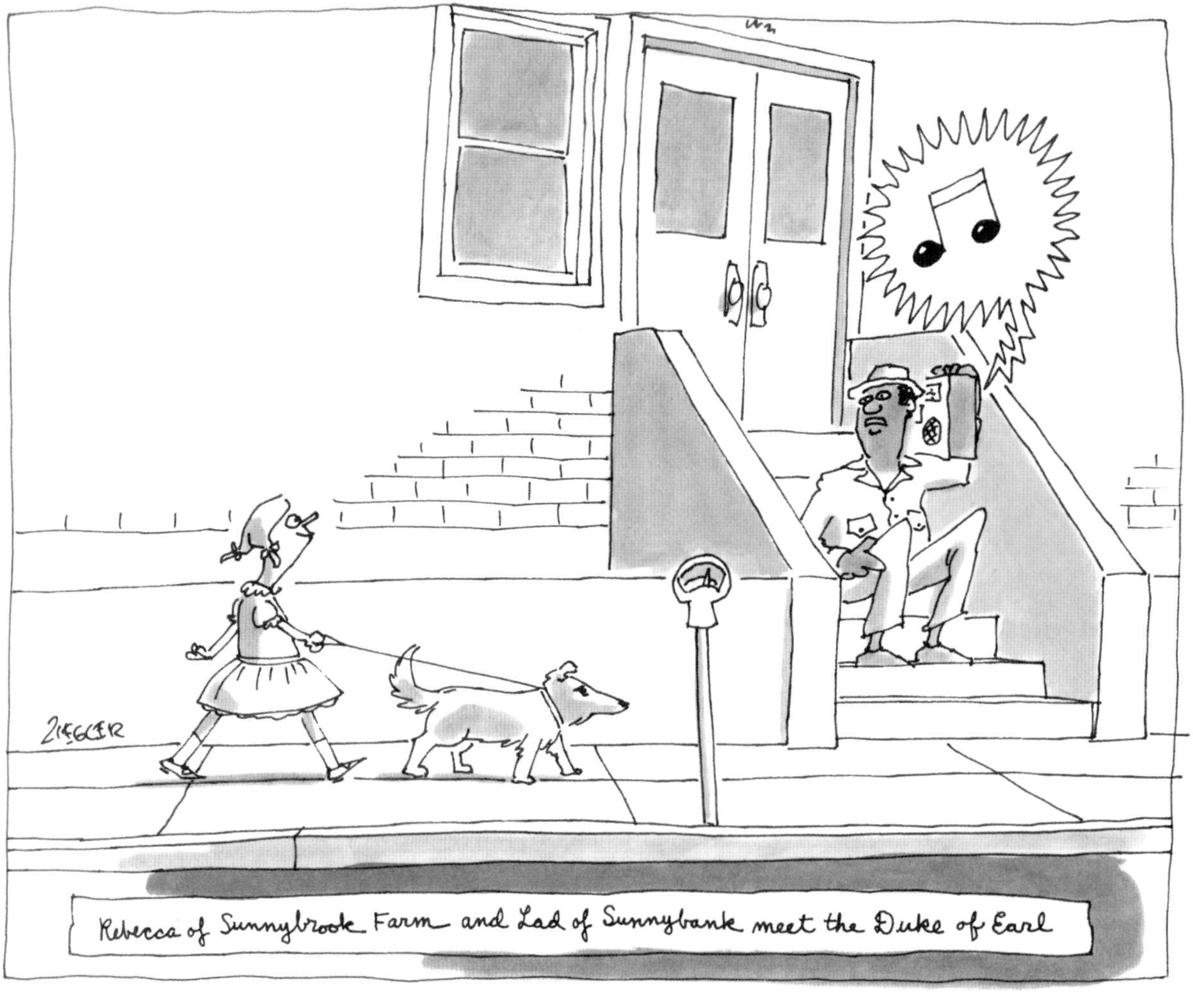
ZIEGLER
Rebecca of Sunnybrook Farm and Lad of Sunnybank meet the Duke of Earl

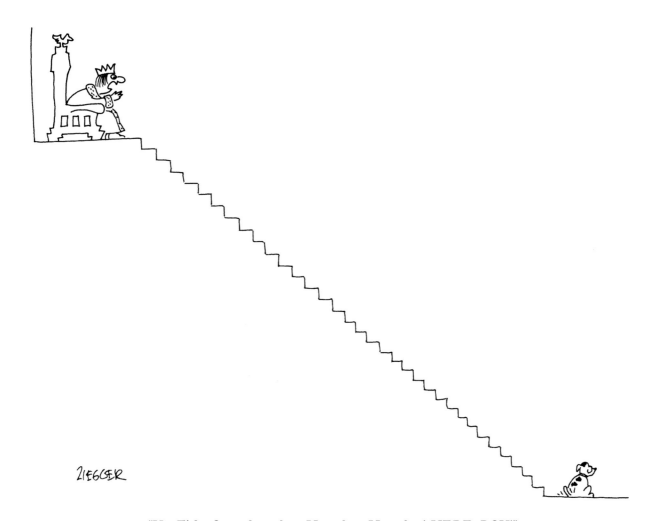

"*Yo, Fido. Come here, boy. Here, boy. Here, boy! HERE, BOY!*"

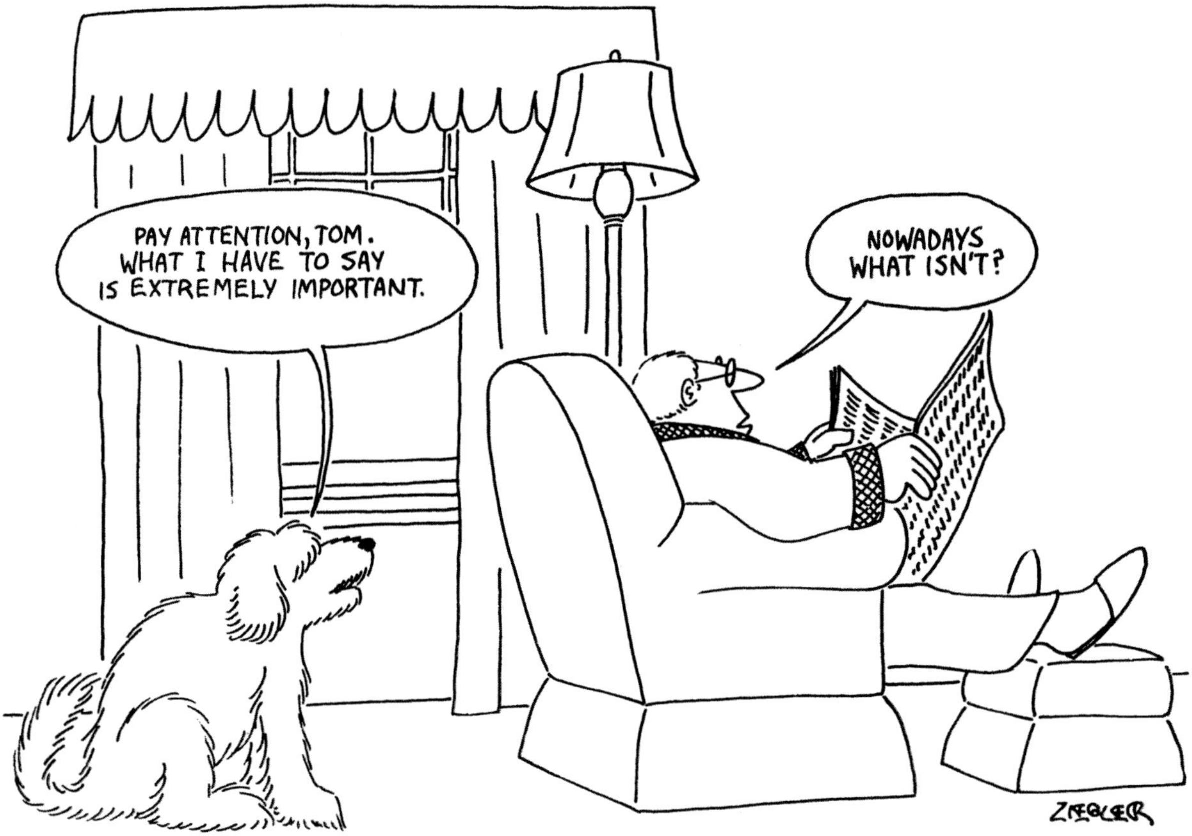
PAY ATTENTION, TOM. WHAT I HAVE TO SAY IS EXTREMELY IMPORTANT.
NOWADAYS WHAT ISN'T?
ZIEGLER

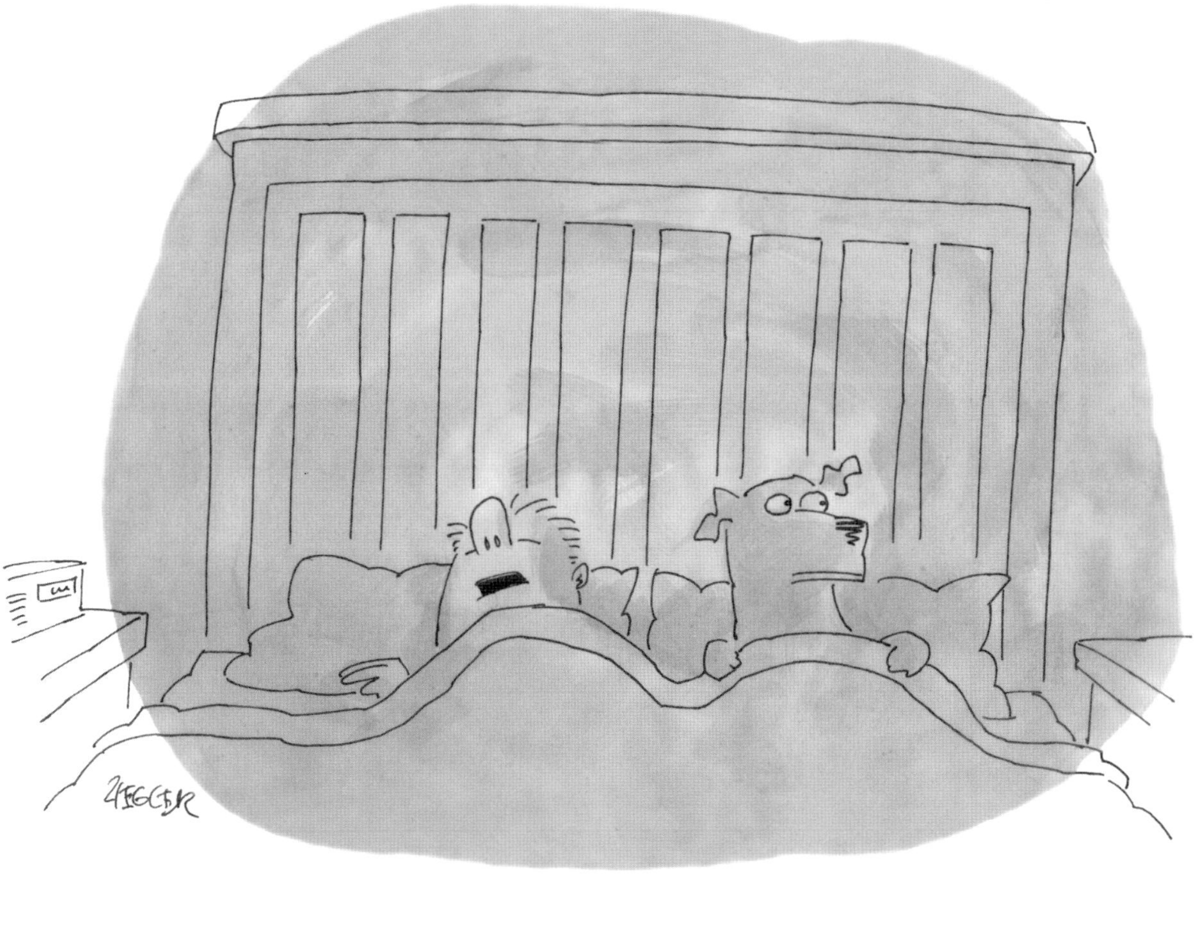
ZIEGLER

"Go back to sleep. It's only the wife."

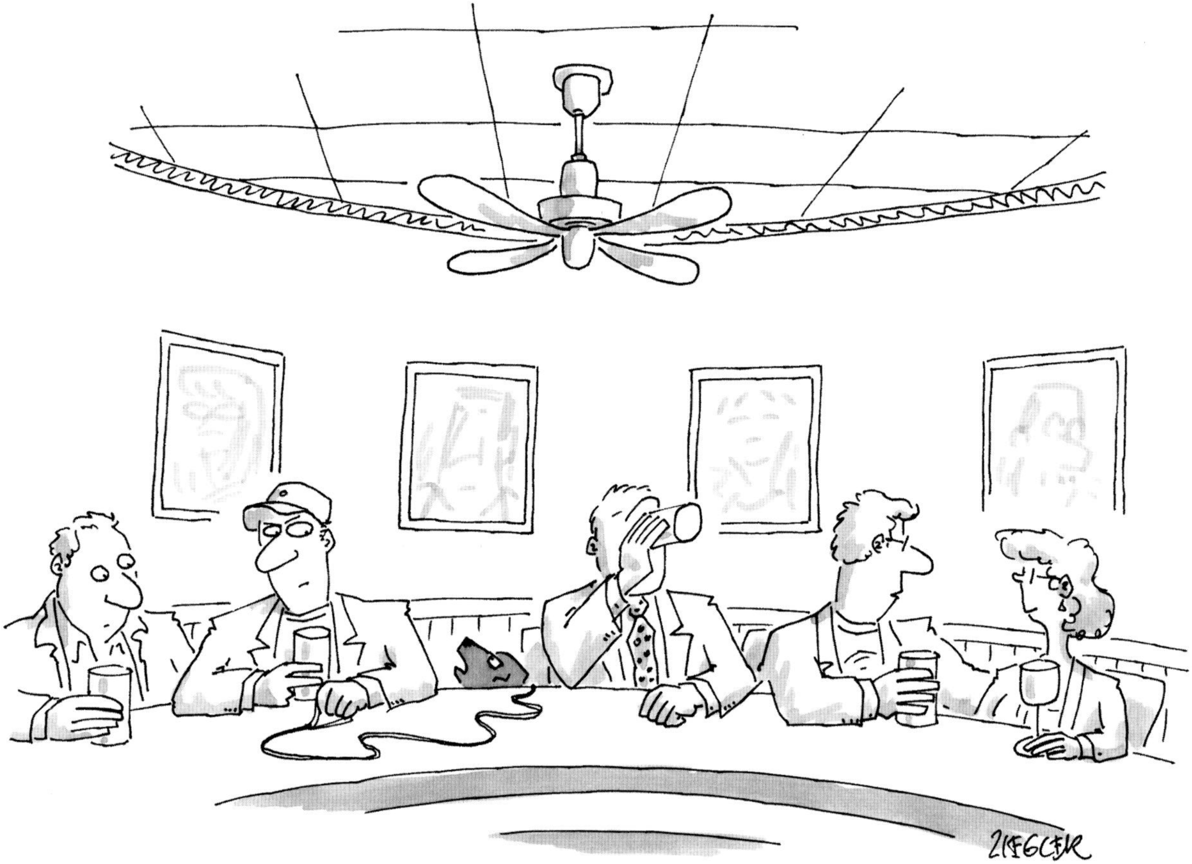
ZIEGLER

"Hey! You call this a walk?"

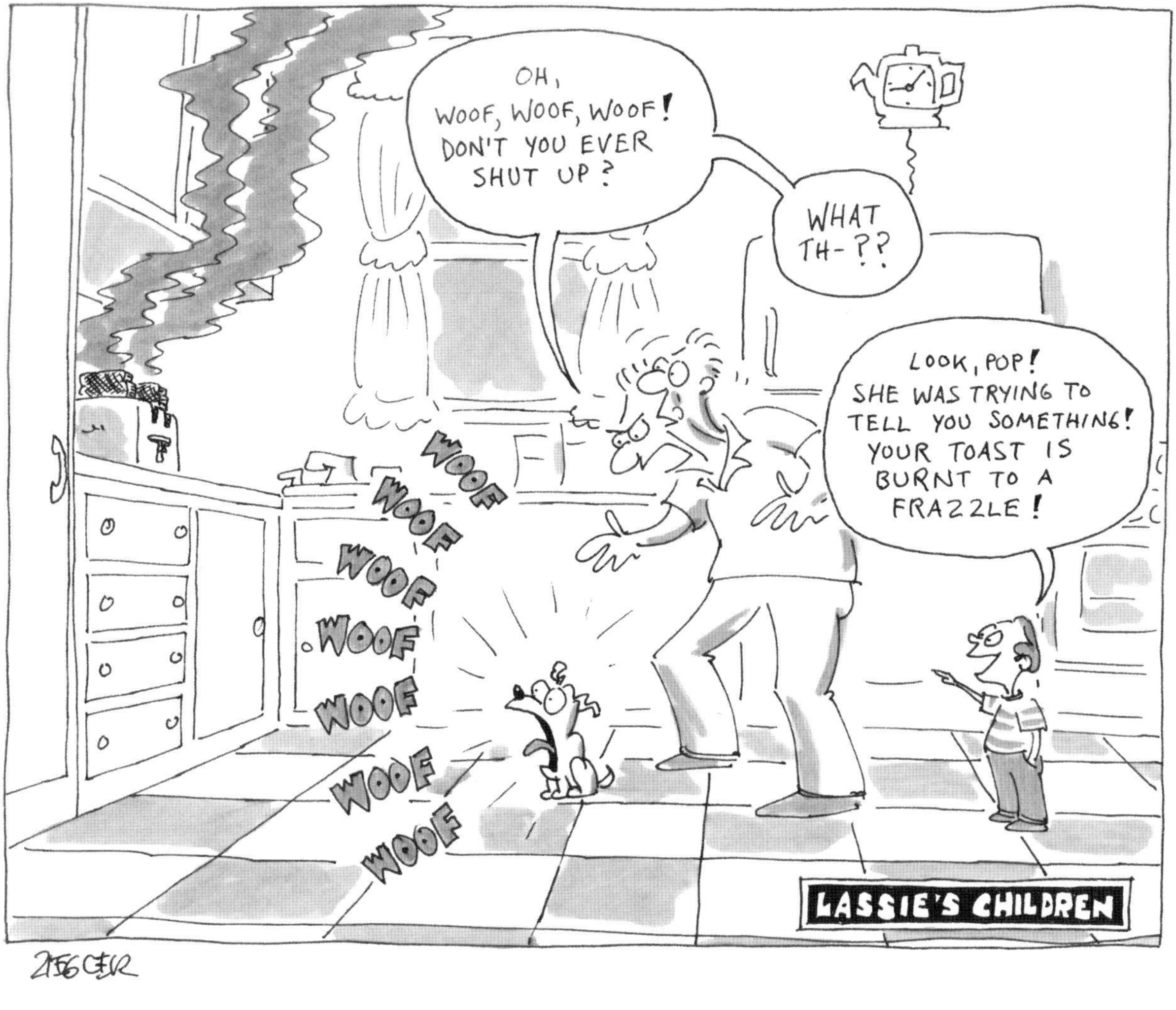
OH,
WOOF, WOOF, WOOF!
DON'T YOU EVER
SHUT UP?
WHAT
TH-??
LOOK, POP!
SHE WAS TRYING TO
TELL YOU SOMETHING!
YOUR TOAST IS
BURNT TO A
FRAZZLE!
WOOF
WOOF
WOOF
WOOF
WOOF
WOOF
WOOF
LASSIE'S CHILDREN
ZIEGLER

"We take Catholic guilt and Jewish guilt for granted. But what of Buddhist and Muslim guilt? Do they exist? Let's start with our definition of guilt."

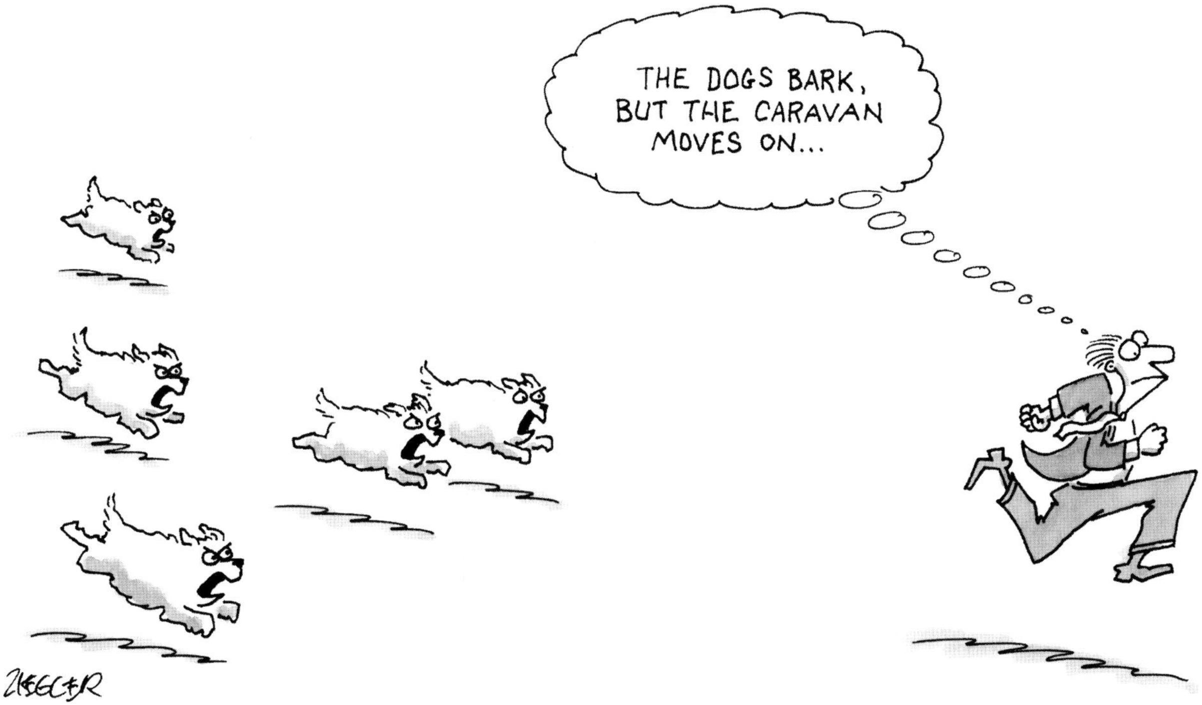
THE DOGS BARK,
BUT THE CARAVAN
MOVES ON...
ZIEGLER

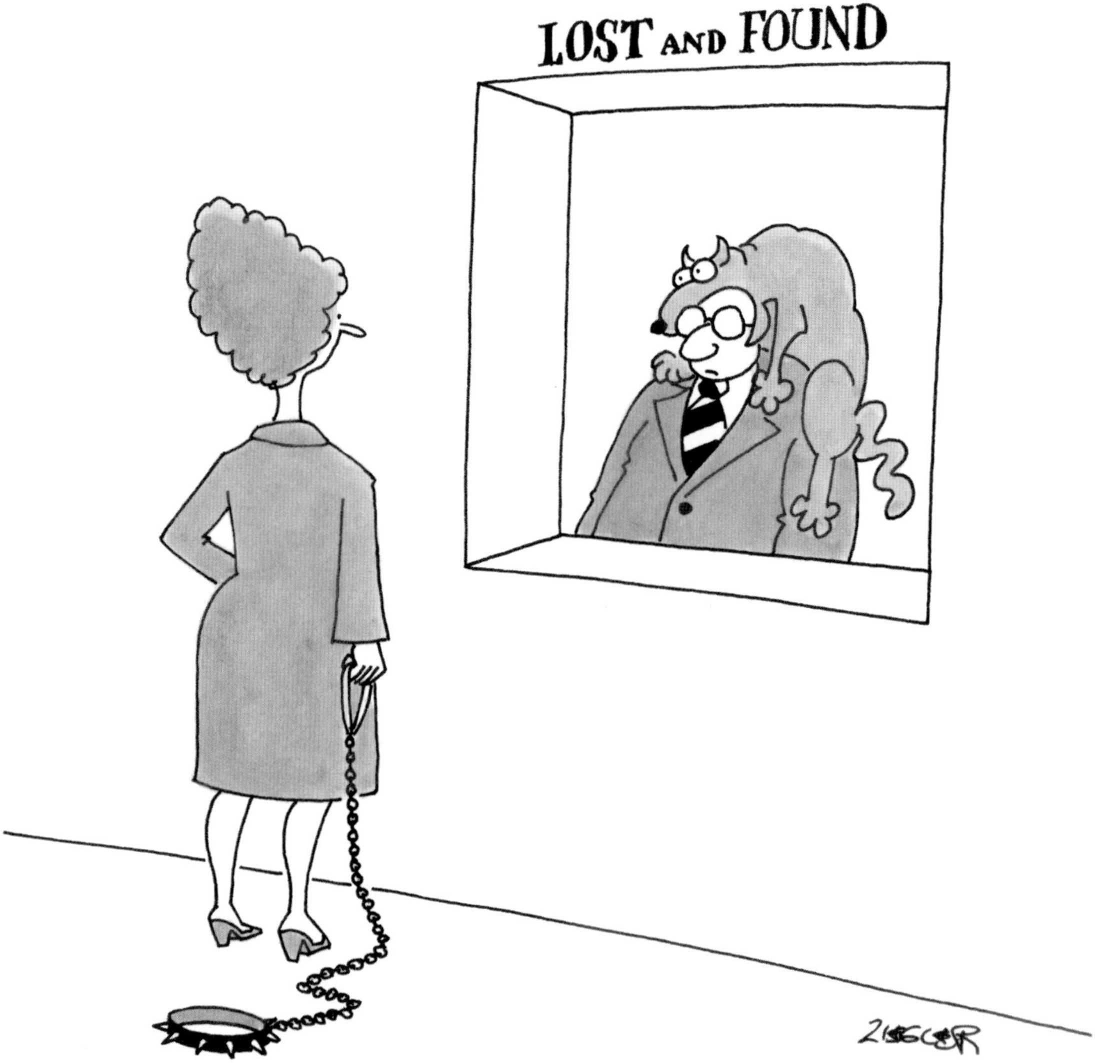
LOST AND FOUND
ZIEGLER

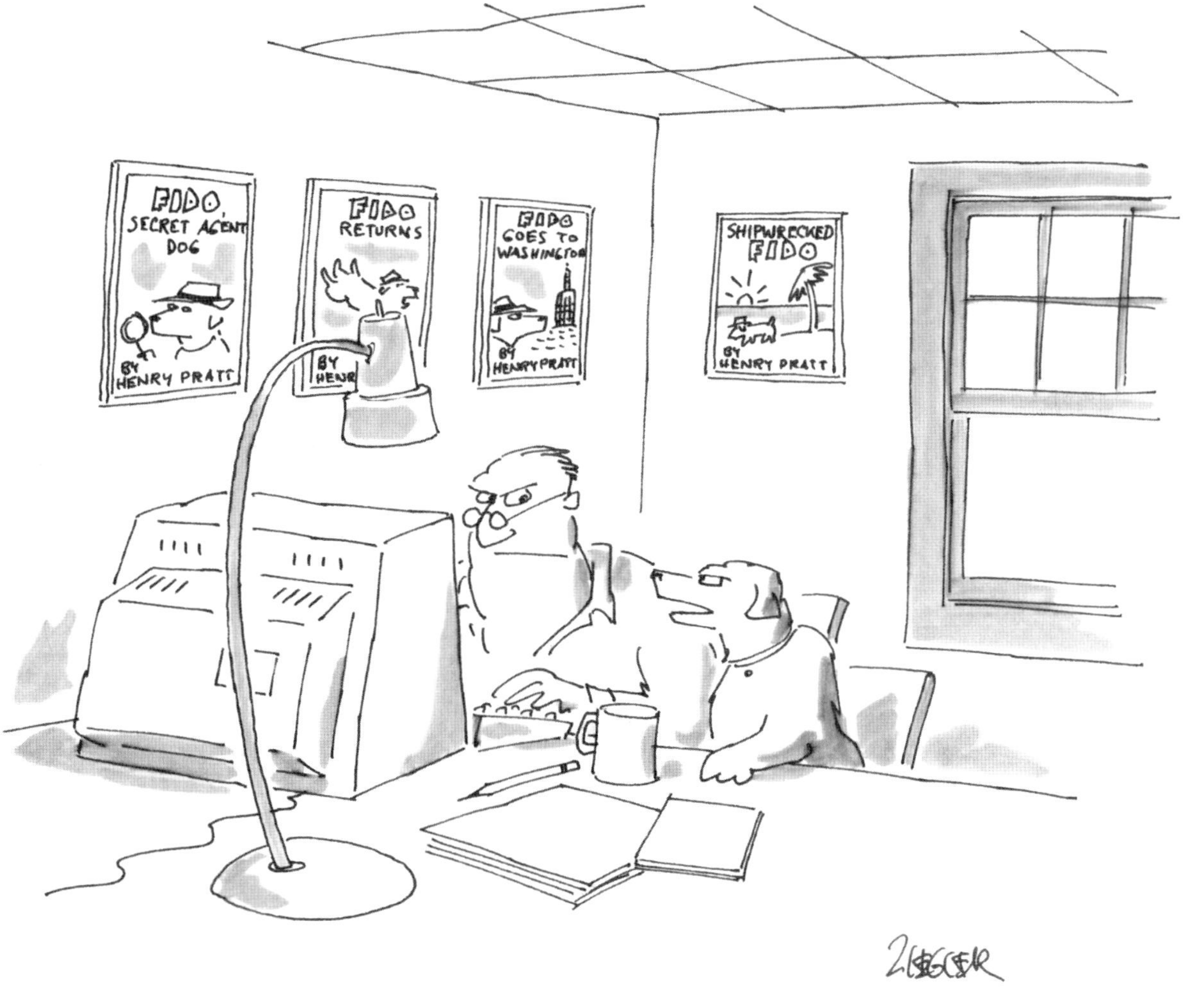
FIDO, SECRET AGENT DOG
BY HENRY PRATT
FIDO RETURNS
FIDO GOES TO WASHINGTON
BY HENRY PRATT
SHIPWRECKED FIDO
BY HENRY PRATT

"Listen to me. I'm a dog and—believe me—a dog would never think, much less act, that way."

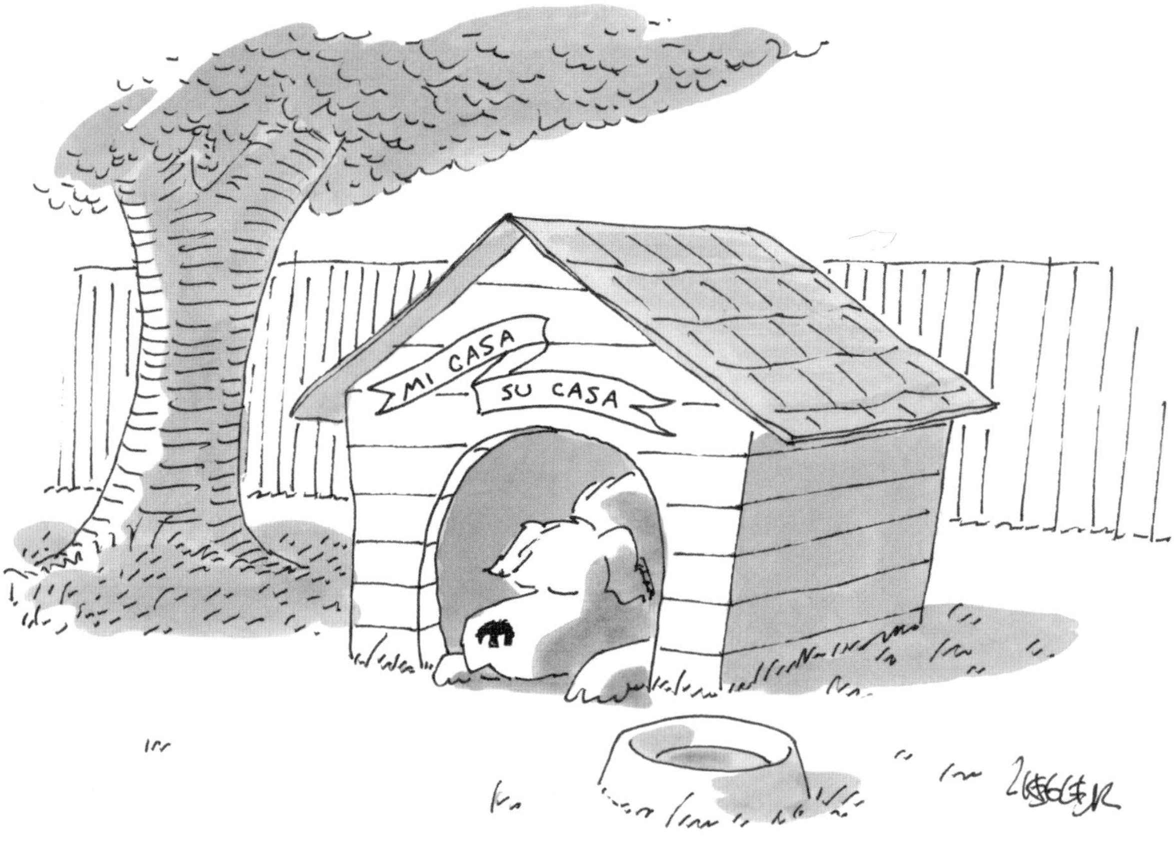
MI CASA
SU CASA

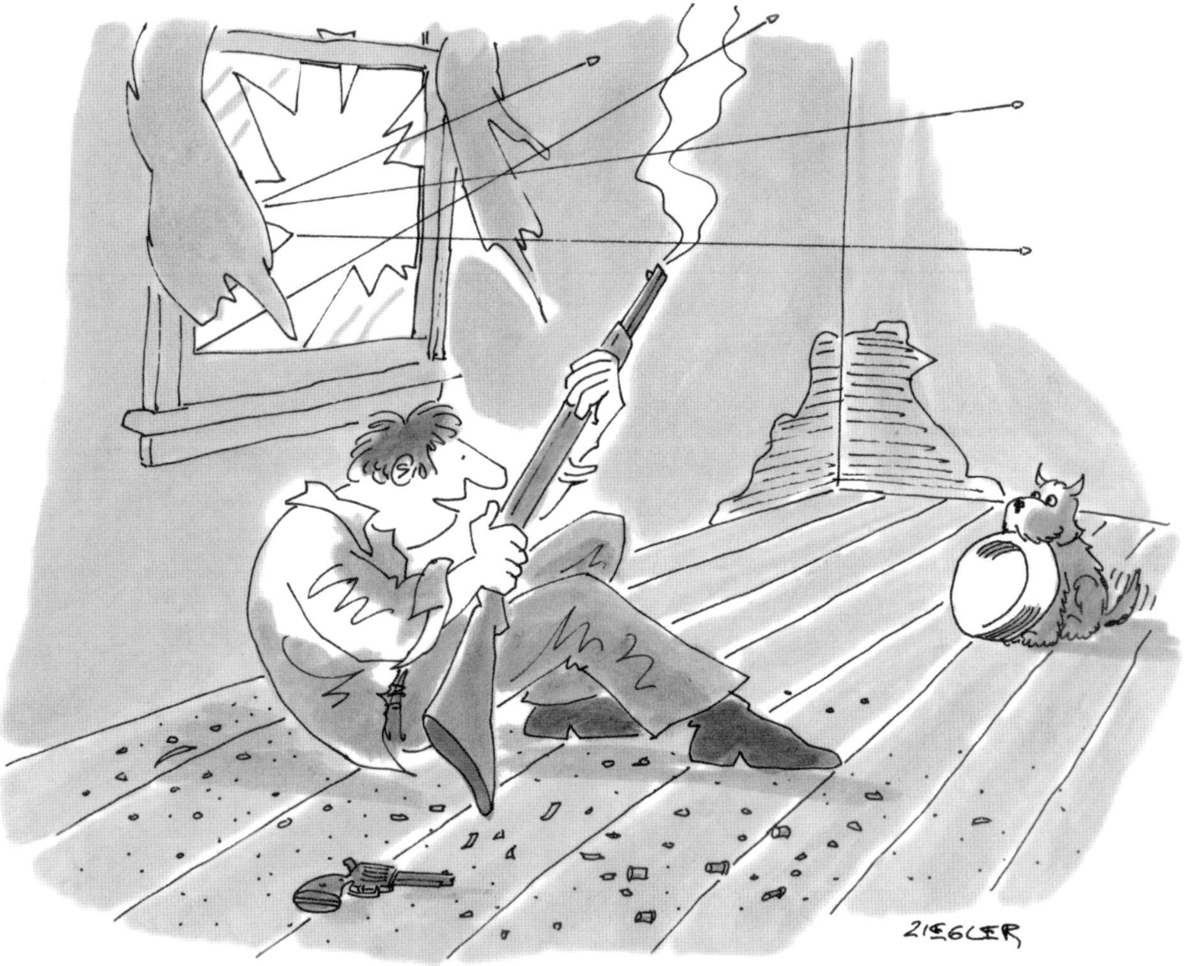
ZIEGLER

"Is wittle Pooka hungwy?"

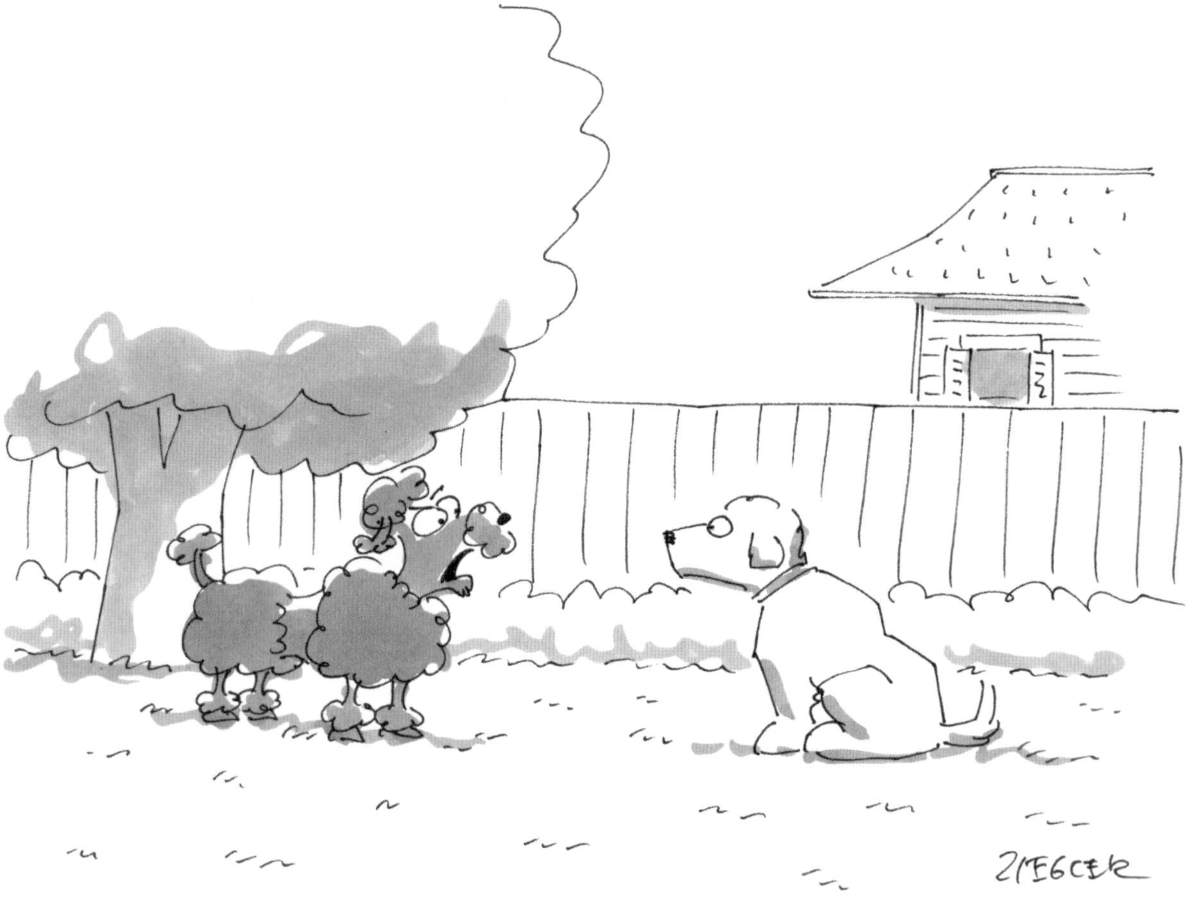
ZIEGLER

"A tick collar? On me?! I don't think so!"

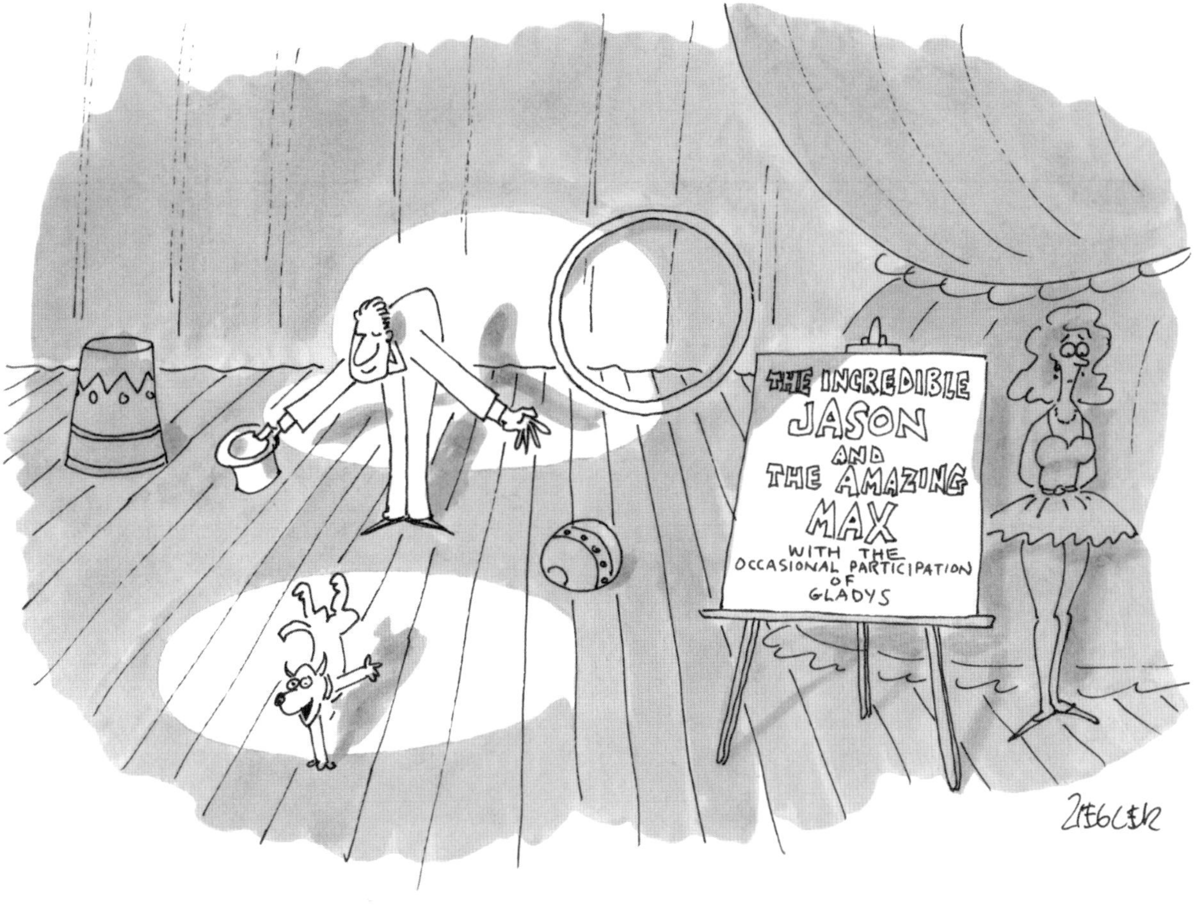
THE INCREDIBLE
JASON
AND
THE AMAZING
MAX
WITH THE
OCCASIONAL PARTICIPATION
OF
GLADYS

"No wonder we could get tickets."

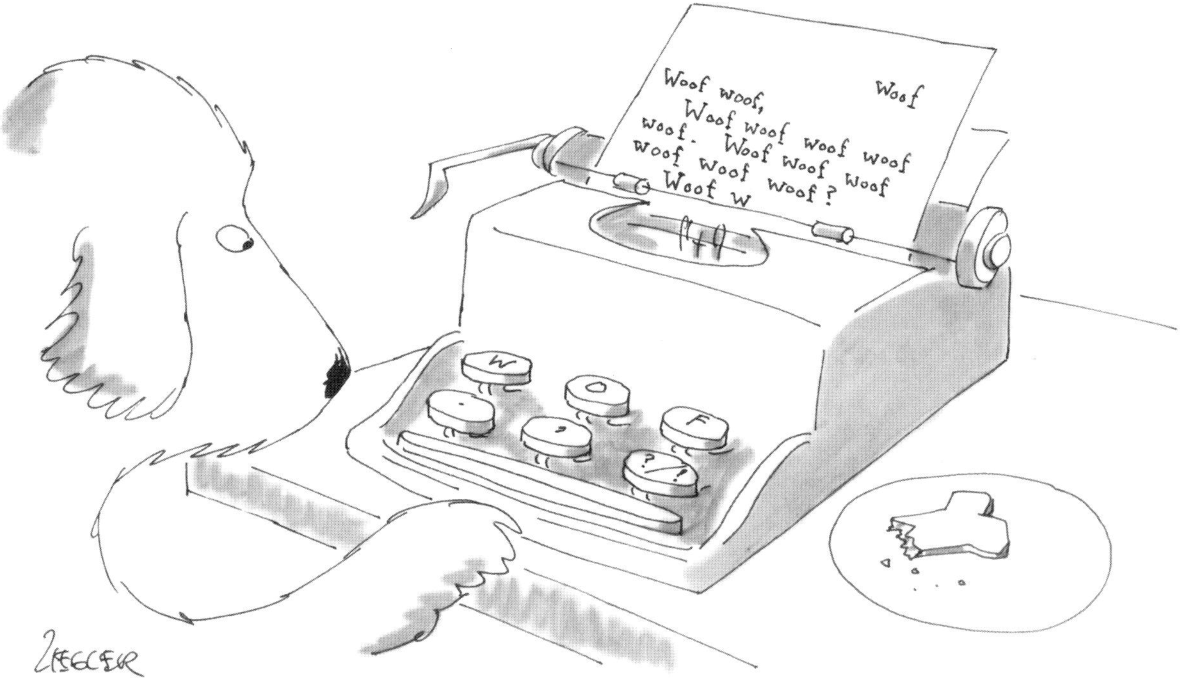
Woof woof, Woof
Woof woof woof woof
woof. Woof woof woof
woof woof woof?
Woof w
W
O
F
?/!

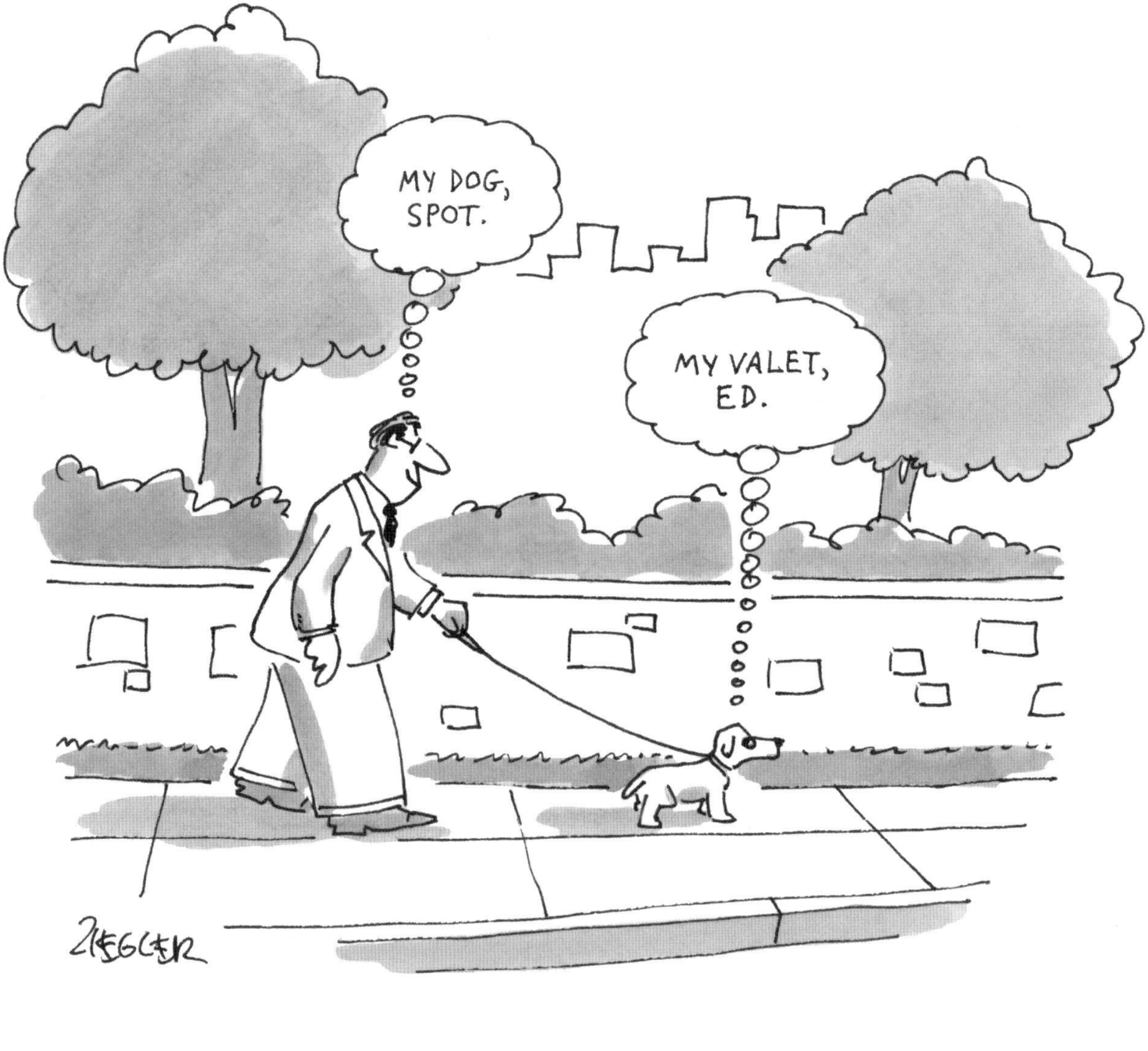
MY DOG, SPOT.
MY VALET, ED.

"For years I've fetched you and fetched you, and have I ever heard a single word of thanks? Have I?

"We walk—sure. But do we talk? No—never!"

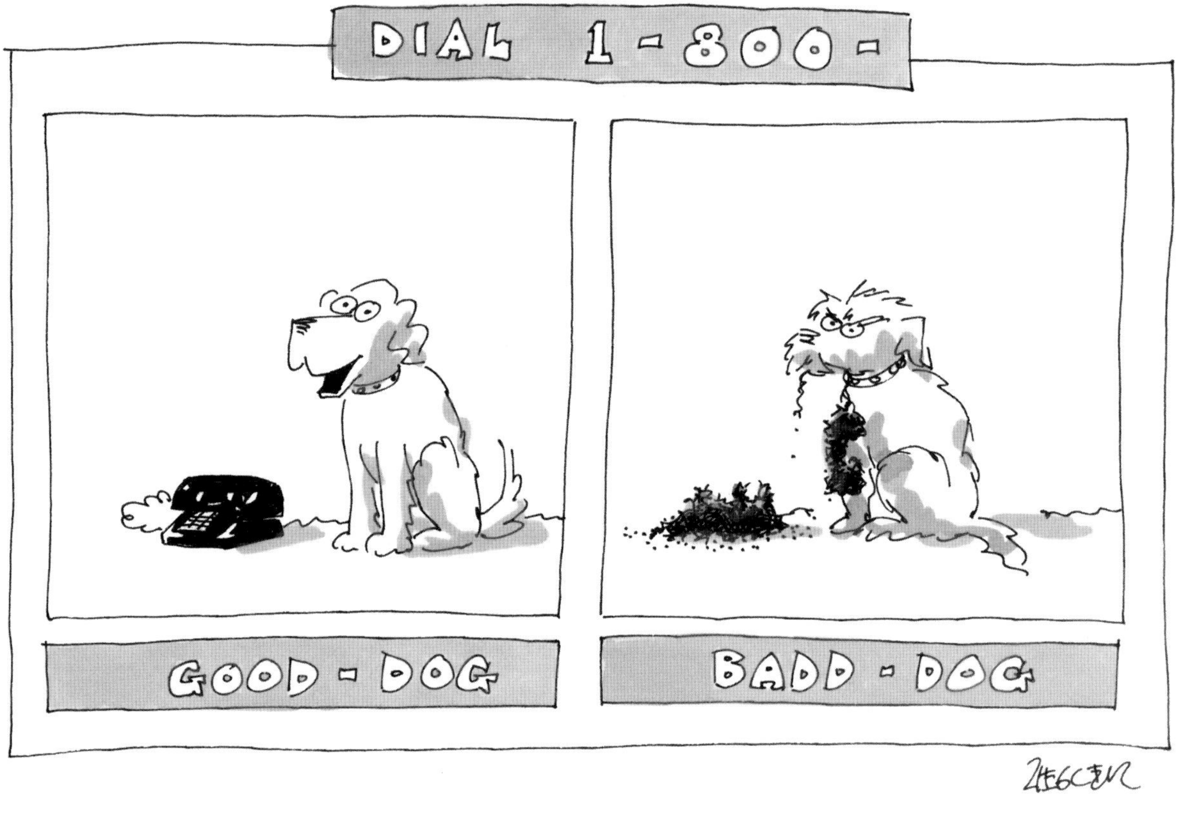
DIAL 1-800-
GOOD-DOG
BADD-DOG
ZIEGLER

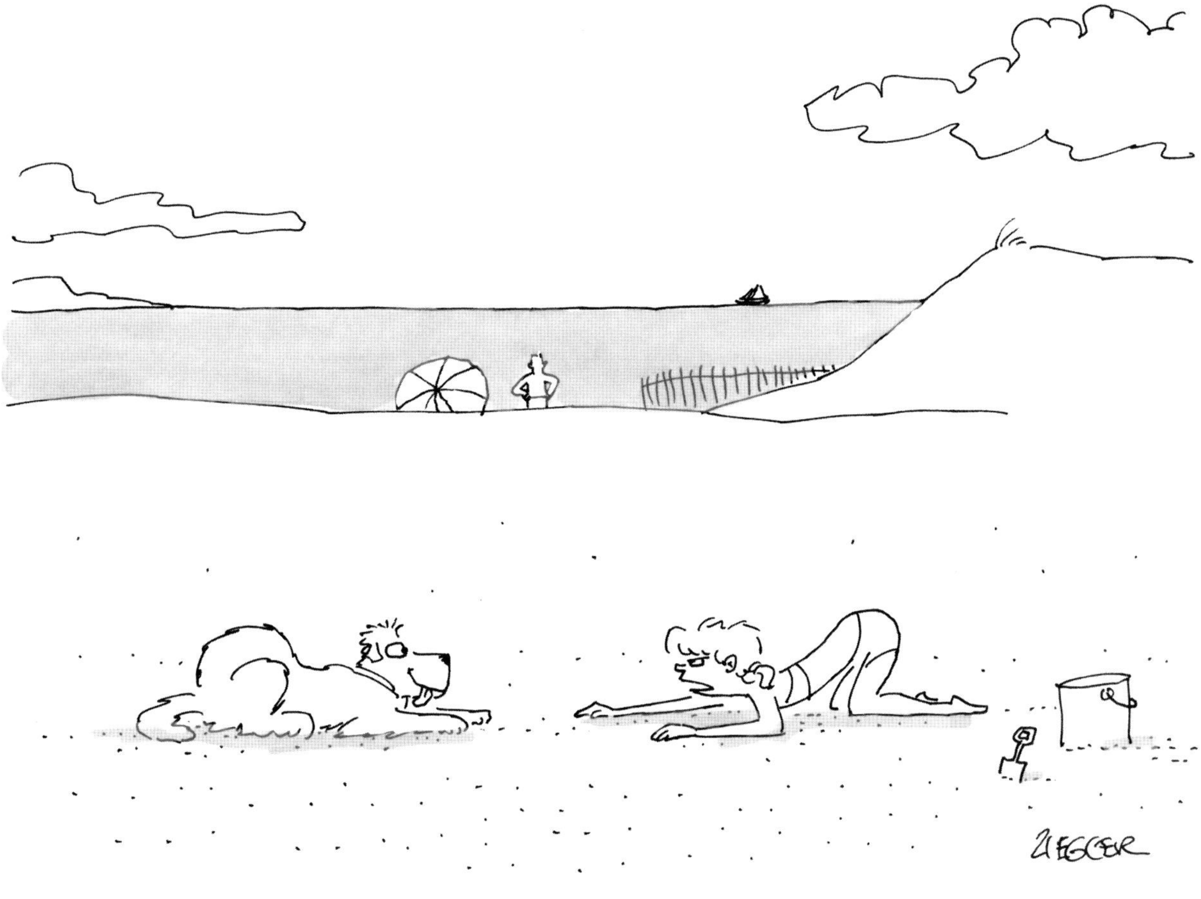
ZIEGLER

"I <u>know</u> you want to play dog! You <u>always</u> want to play dog!"

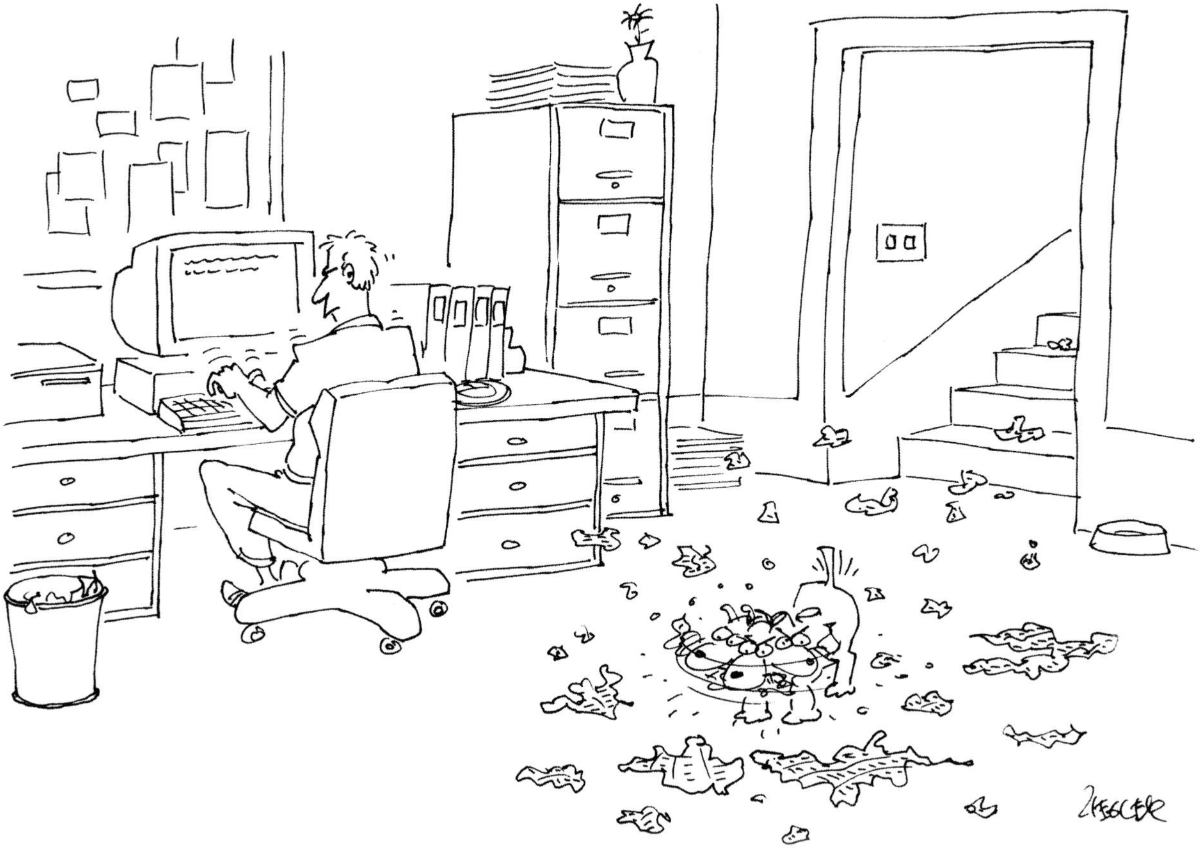
ZIEGLER

As I have long suspected, a glitch in my present information retrieval system sometimes allows it to slip into the destruct mode."

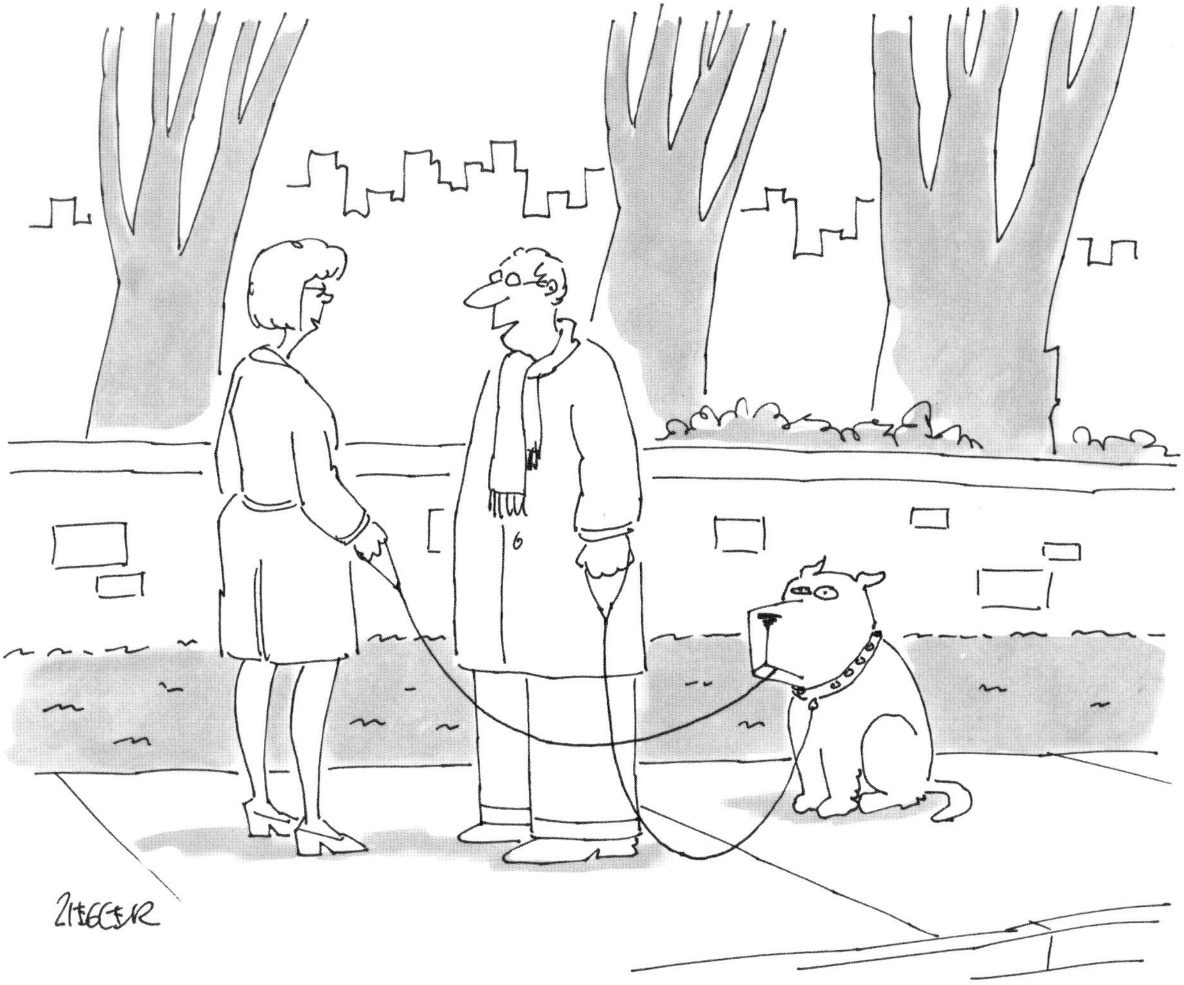
ZIEGLER

Oprah and Dr. Phil have a certain gusto, I suppose, but
they lack the sheer problem-solving bravado of a Rin-Tin-Tin."

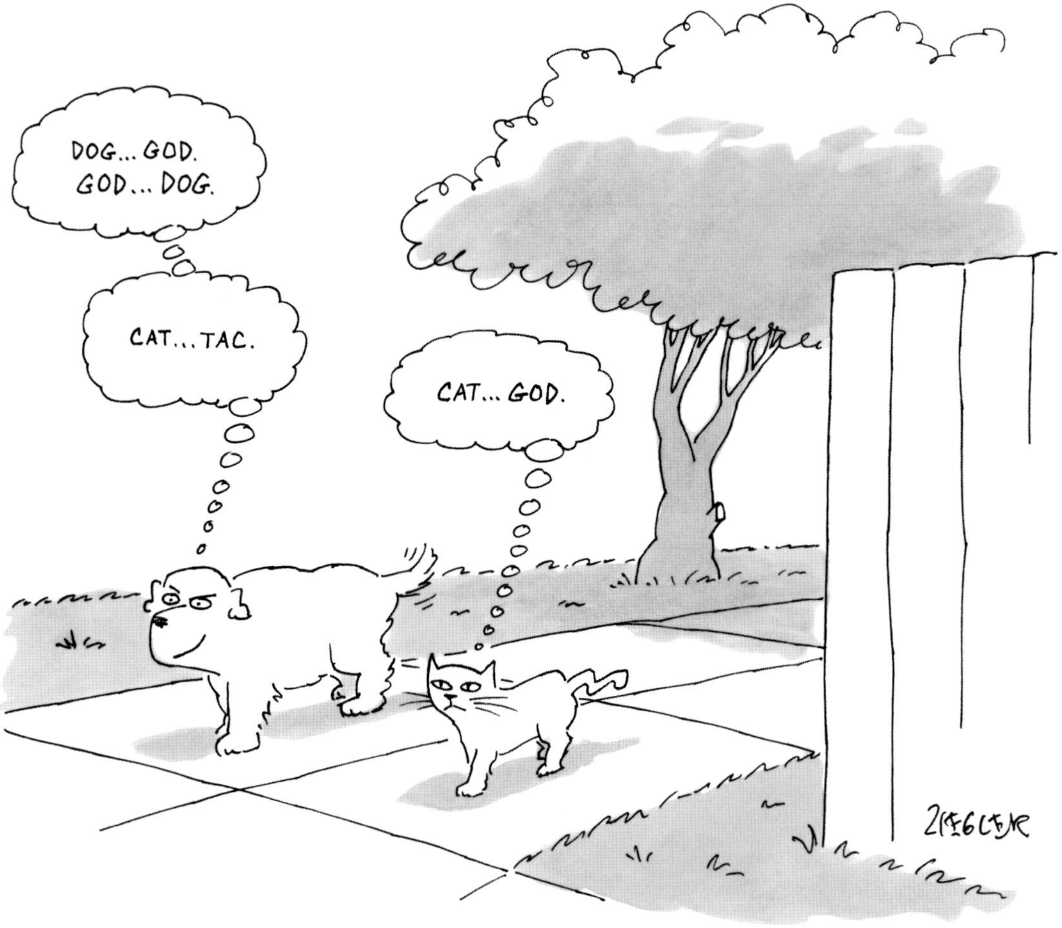
DOG... GOD.
GOD... DOG.
CAT... TAC.
CAT... GOD.

"No, I do <u>not</u> want to do it doggie-style."